C-341 CAREER EXAMINATION SERIES

This is your
PASSBOOK for...

Housing Manager

Test Preparation Study Guide
Questions & Answers

COPYRIGHT NOTICE

This book is SOLELY intended for, is sold ONLY to, and its use is RESTRICTED to individual, bona fide applicants or candidates who qualify by virtue of having seriously filed applications for appropriate license, certificate, professional and/or promotional advancement, higher school matriculation, scholarship, or other legitimate requirements of education and/or governmental authorities.

This book is NOT intended for use, class instruction, tutoring, training, duplication, copying, reprinting, excerption, or adaptation, etc., by:

1) Other publishers
2) Proprietors and/or Instructors of "Coaching" and/or Preparatory Courses
3) Personnel and/or Training Divisions of commercial, industrial, and governmental organizations
4) Schools, colleges, or universities and/or their departments and staffs, including teachers and other personnel
5) Testing Agencies or Bureaus
6) Study groups which seek by the purchase of a single volume to copy and/or duplicate and/or adapt this material for use by the group as a whole without having purchased individual volumes for each of the members of the group
7) Et al.

Such persons would be in violation of appropriate Federal and State statutes.

PROVISION OF LICENSING AGREEMENTS – Recognized educational, commercial, industrial, and governmental institutions and organizations, and others legitimately engaged in educational pursuits, including training, testing, and measurement activities, may address request for a licensing agreement to the copyright owners, who will determine whether, and under what conditions, including fees and charges, the materials in this book may be used them. In other words, a licensing facility exists for the legitimate use of the material in this book on other than an individual basis. However, it is asseverated and affirmed here that the material in this book CANNOT be used without the receipt of the express permission of such a licensing agreement from the Publishers. Inquiries re licensing should be addressed to the company, attention rights and permissions department.

All rights reserved, including the right of reproduction in whole or in part, in any form or by any means, electronic or mechanical, including photocopying, recording, or by any information storage and retrieval system, without permission in writing from the Publisher.

Copyright © 2024 by
National Learning Corporation

212 Michael Drive, Syosset, NY 11791
(516) 921-8888 • www.passbooks.com
E-mail: info@passbooks.com

PUBLISHED IN THE UNITED STATES OF AMERICA

PASSBOOK® SERIES

THE *PASSBOOK® SERIES* has been created to prepare applicants and candidates for the ultimate academic battlefield – the examination room.

At some time in our lives, each and every one of us may be required to take an examination – for validation, matriculation, admission, qualification, registration, certification, or licensure.

Based on the assumption that every applicant or candidate has met the basic formal educational standards, has taken the required number of courses, and read the necessary texts, the *PASSBOOK® SERIES* furnishes the one special preparation which may assure passing with confidence, instead of failing with insecurity. Examination questions – together with answers – are furnished as the basic vehicle for study so that the mysteries of the examination and its compounding difficulties may be eliminated or diminished by a sure method.

This book is meant to help you pass your examination provided that you qualify and are serious in your objective.

The entire field is reviewed through the huge store of content information which is succinctly presented through a provocative and challenging approach – the question-and-answer method.

A climate of success is established by furnishing the correct answers at the end of each test.

You soon learn to recognize types of questions, forms of questions, and patterns of questioning. You may even begin to anticipate expected outcomes.

You perceive that many questions are repeated or adapted so that you can gain acute insights, which may enable you to score many sure points.

You learn how to confront new questions, or types of questions, and to attack them confidently and work out the correct answers.

You note objectives and emphases, and recognize pitfalls and dangers, so that you may make positive educational adjustments.

Moreover, you are kept fully informed in relation to new concepts, methods, practices, and directions in the field.

You discover that you are actually taking the examination all the time: you are preparing for the examination by "taking" an examination, not by reading extraneous and/or supererogatory textbooks.

In short, this PASSBOOK®, used directedly, should be an important factor in helping you to pass your test.

HOUSING MANAGER

DUTIES:
Housing Manger, under general direction, perform difficult and responsible work in the administration and management of Housing Authority's public housing programs; manage a large housing development or a number of small developments or scattered site buildings and supervise the staff of said facilities; manage the maintenance/repair of the physical plant, and the handling of tenant and community relations; oversee the process of determining eligibility for public housing and/or leased housing programs; assign apartments; ensure the accuracy and timeliness of the development's financial records; develop budget estimates for development operation; monitor operational expenditures, including overtime usage, purchasing, initiating of new contracts and usage of existing contracts; inspect housing development properties; monitor the progress and quality of work performed by private contractors; secure public and private agency cooperation; may supervise the operation of an administrative unit or act as staff assistant to an Authority executive. All Housing Managers perform related work.

SCOPE OF THE EXAMINATION:
The multiple-choice test is designed to assess the extent to which candidates have certain abilities determined to be important to the performance of the tasks of a Housing Manager. Task areas to be tested are as follows: Rent Collection; Annual Review and Turnover; Maintenance; Social and Community Services; Tenant Relations; Contract Administration; Supervision of Staff; Administrative Duties; and Standards of Proper Employee Ethical Conduct.

The test may include questions which require the use of any of the following abilities:
1. **Analytical Thinking**: Analyzing information and using logic to address specific work-related issues and problems; involves the identification of problems, not implementation of solutions. Example: A Housing Manager might use this ability when identifying that there is not enough staff to complete the duties of the day.
2. **Quantitative Analysis and Interpretation**: Interpreting and understanding the underlying principles and meaning of numerical data; recognizing inconsistencies and errors in reports containing numerical data. May involve making projections. Example: A Housing Manager might use this ability when making budget projections for the year.
3. **Planning and Organizing**: Establishing a method of execution to accomplish a specific goal over an extended period of time; determining appropriate assignments and allocation of resources. Example: A Housing Manager might use this ability when assigning the appropriate number of staff to a project.
4. **Judgement and Decision-Making**: Reviewing information to develop and evaluate the relative costs and benefits of potential solutions to problems and choosing the most appropriate one; implementing a course of action determined by thinking analytically. While similar to Planning and Organizing, Judgement and Decision Making are typically applied over a shorter time frame. Example: A Housing Manager might use this ability when facilitating a solution for a problem such as a pipe bursting.
5. **Management of Financial Resources**: Determining how money will be spent to get the work done and accounting for these expenditures; managing the money needed for getting work accomplished. Example: A Housing Manager might use this ability when allocating funds to the appropriate budget areas.
6. **Management of Material Resources**: Obtaining and seeing to the appropriate use of equipment facilities and materials needed to do certain work; managing the things needed for work to be accomplished. Example: A Housing Manager might use this ability when determining whether purchased materials are of appropriate size, function and number to meet the housing development needs.

7. **Management of Personnel Resources**: Motivating, developing and directing people as they work, identifying the best people for the job; managing employees needed to accomplish tasks. Example: A Housing Manager might use this ability when determining the most knowledgeable and articulate housing assistant to appear in court for a hearing.
8. **Monitoring**: Monitoring/assessing performance of oneself, other individuals or organizations to make improvements or take corrective action; overseeing the quality of performance. Example: A Housing Manager might use this ability when conducting a performance review for their direct report.
9. **Adaptability/Flexibility**: Responding to change (positive or negative) in a constructive manner and adapting an approach as needed to the situation. Example: A Housing Manager might use this ability when redistributing work when an employee is absent.
10. **Written Expression**: Appropriately communicating information and ideas presented in written words and sentences so intended audience will understand. Example: A Housing Manager might use this ability when drafting email correspondence to the Resident Association.
11. **Persuading and Influencing Others**: Causing others to change or modify their opinions, views or behaviors using a variety of strategies. Example: A Housing Manager might use this ability when initiating disciplinary action for a staff member.
12. **Conflict Resolution**: Negotiating with others to resolve grievances or conflicts and handle complaints by developing a constructive solution. Example: A Housing Manager might use this ability when addressing interpersonal disputes amongst staff.
13. **Concern for Others**: Acting in a manner sensitive to others' needs and feelings while being understanding and helpful on the job; showing consideration. Example: A Housing Manager might use this ability when discussing an employee's personal issues that may be affecting work performance.
14. **Coaching and Mentoring**: Identifying the developmental needs of others and coaching, mentoring, or otherwise helping others to improve their knowledge or skills. Example: A Housing Manager might use this ability when recommending an employee to useful training resources to improve their productivity.
15. **Teamwork**: Developing mutual trust and cooperation while working together towards the accomplishment of a common goal or outcome. Example: A Housing Manager might use this ability when updating other team members at each phase of a project.
16. **Integrity**: Acting in an honest and ethical manner. Example: A Housing Manager might use this ability when refusing a bribe (offered from a third-party vendor) and following the proper protocols to report it.
17. **Dependability**: Fulfilling obligations and acting in a reliable, responsible and dependable manner. Example: A Housing Manager might use this ability when promptly completing reports requested by the Borough Office.
18. **Achievement/Effort**: Establishing and maintaining personally challenging achievement goals and exerting effort toward mastering tasks to reach set goals. Example: A Housing Manager might use this ability when working toward decreasing their delinquency score.
19. **Initiative and Independence**: Displaying a willingness to take on additional responsibilities and challenges, while developing one's own ways of doing things and guiding oneself with little or no supervision. Example: A Housing Manager might use this ability when taking on the responsibilities of a staff member who is out sick.
20. **Attention to Detail**: Being careful about details and thorough in completing work tasks. Example: A Housing Manager might use this ability when preparing court documents for a hearing.
21. **Updating and Using Relevant Knowledge**: Keeping up-to-date technically and applying new knowledge to the job. Example: A Housing Manager might use this ability when studying a new online review system.

HOW TO TAKE A TEST

I. YOU MUST PASS AN EXAMINATION

A. *WHAT EVERY CANDIDATE SHOULD KNOW*

Examination applicants often ask us for help in preparing for the written test. What can I study in advance? What kinds of questions will be asked? How will the test be given? How will the papers be graded?

As an applicant for a civil service examination, you may be wondering about some of these things. Our purpose here is to suggest effective methods of advance study and to describe civil service examinations.

Your chances for success on this examination can be increased if you know how to prepare. Those "pre-examination jitters" can be reduced if you know what to expect. You can even experience an adventure in good citizenship if you know why civil service exams are given.

B. *WHY ARE CIVIL SERVICE EXAMINATIONS GIVEN?*

Civil service examinations are important to you in two ways. As a citizen, you want public jobs filled by employees who know how to do their work. As a job seeker, you want a fair chance to compete for that job on an equal footing with other candidates. The best-known means of accomplishing this two-fold goal is the competitive examination.

Exams are widely publicized throughout the nation. They may be administered for jobs in federal, state, city, municipal, town or village governments or agencies.

Any citizen may apply, with some limitations, such as the age or residence of applicants. Your experience and education may be reviewed to see whether you meet the requirements for the particular examination. When these requirements exist, they are reasonable and applied consistently to all applicants. Thus, a competitive examination may cause you some uneasiness now, but it is your privilege and safeguard.

C. *HOW ARE CIVIL SERVICE EXAMS DEVELOPED?*

Examinations are carefully written by trained technicians who are specialists in the field known as "psychological measurement," in consultation with recognized authorities in the field of work that the test will cover. These experts recommend the subject matter areas or skills to be tested; only those knowledges or skills important to your success on the job are included. The most reliable books and source materials available are used as references. Together, the experts and technicians judge the difficulty level of the questions.

Test technicians know how to phrase questions so that the problem is clearly stated. Their ethics do not permit "trick" or "catch" questions. Questions may have been tried out on sample groups, or subjected to statistical analysis, to determine their usefulness.

Written tests are often used in combination with performance tests, ratings of training and experience, and oral interviews. All of these measures combine to form the best-known means of finding the right person for the right job.

II. HOW TO PASS THE WRITTEN TEST

A. NATURE OF THE EXAMINATION

To prepare intelligently for civil service examinations, you should know how they differ from school examinations you have taken. In school you were assigned certain definite pages to read or subjects to cover. The examination questions were quite detailed and usually emphasized memory. Civil service exams, on the other hand, try to discover your present ability to perform the duties of a position, plus your potentiality to learn these duties. In other words, a civil service exam attempts to predict how successful you will be. Questions cover such a broad area that they cannot be as minute and detailed as school exam questions.

In the public service similar kinds of work, or positions, are grouped together in one "class." This process is known as *position-classification*. All the positions in a class are paid according to the salary range for that class. One class title covers all of these positions, and they are all tested by the same examination.

B. FOUR BASIC STEPS

1) Study the announcement

How, then, can you know what subjects to study? Our best answer is: "Learn as much as possible about the class of positions for which you've applied." The exam will test the knowledge, skills and abilities needed to do the work.

Your most valuable source of information about the position you want is the official exam announcement. This announcement lists the training and experience qualifications. Check these standards and apply only if you come reasonably close to meeting them.

The brief description of the position in the examination announcement offers some clues to the subjects which will be tested. Think about the job itself. Review the duties in your mind. Can you perform them, or are there some in which you are rusty? Fill in the blank spots in your preparation.

Many jurisdictions preview the written test in the exam announcement by including a section called "Knowledge and Abilities Required," "Scope of the Examination," or some similar heading. Here you will find out specifically what fields will be tested.

2) Review your own background

Once you learn in general what the position is all about, and what you need to know to do the work, ask yourself which subjects you already know fairly well and which need improvement. You may wonder whether to concentrate on improving your strong areas or on building some background in your fields of weakness. When the announcement has specified "some knowledge" or "considerable knowledge," or has used adjectives like "beginning principles of..." or "advanced ... methods," you can get a clue as to the number and difficulty of questions to be asked in any given field. More questions, and hence broader coverage, would be included for those subjects which are more important in the work. Now weigh your strengths and weaknesses against the job requirements and prepare accordingly.

3) Determine the level of the position

Another way to tell how intensively you should prepare is to understand the level of the job for which you are applying. Is it the entering level? In other words, is this the position in which beginners in a field of work are hired? Or is it an intermediate or advanced level? Sometimes this is indicated by such words as "Junior" or "Senior" in the class title. Other jurisdictions use Roman numerals to designate the level – Clerk I, Clerk II, for example. The word "Supervisor" sometimes appears in the title. If the level is not indicated by the title, check the description of duties. Will you be working under very close supervision, or will you have responsibility for independent decisions in this work?

4) Choose appropriate study materials

Now that you know the subjects to be examined and the relative amount of each subject to be covered, you can choose suitable study materials. For beginning level jobs, or even advanced ones, if you have a pronounced weakness in some aspect of your training, read a modern, standard textbook in that field. Be sure it is up to date and has general coverage. Such books are normally available at your library, and the librarian will be glad to help you locate one. For entry-level positions, questions of appropriate difficulty are chosen -- neither highly advanced questions, nor those too simple. Such questions require careful thought but not advanced training.

If the position for which you are applying is technical or advanced, you will read more advanced, specialized material. If you are already familiar with the basic principles of your field, elementary textbooks would waste your time. Concentrate on advanced textbooks and technical periodicals. Think through the concepts and review difficult problems in your field.

These are all general sources. You can get more ideas on your own initiative, following these leads. For example, training manuals and publications of the government agency which employs workers in your field can be useful, particularly for technical and professional positions. A letter or visit to the government department involved may result in more specific study suggestions, and certainly will provide you with a more definite idea of the exact nature of the position you are seeking.

III. KINDS OF TESTS

Tests are used for purposes other than measuring knowledge and ability to perform specified duties. For some positions, it is equally important to test ability to make adjustments to new situations or to profit from training. In others, basic mental abilities not dependent on information are essential. Questions which test these things may not appear as pertinent to the duties of the position as those which test for knowledge and information. Yet they are often highly important parts of a fair examination. For very general questions, it is almost impossible to help you direct your study efforts. What we can do is to point out some of the more common of these general abilities needed in public service positions and describe some typical questions.

1) General information

Broad, general information has been found useful for predicting job success in some kinds of work. This is tested in a variety of ways, from vocabulary lists to questions about current events. Basic background in some field of work, such as sociology or economics, may be sampled in a group of questions. Often these are principles which have become familiar to most persons through exposure rather than through formal training. It is difficult to advise you how to study for these questions; being alert to the world around you is our best suggestion.

2) Verbal ability

An example of an ability needed in many positions is verbal or language ability. Verbal ability is, in brief, the ability to use and understand words. Vocabulary and grammar tests are typical measures of this ability. Reading comprehension or paragraph interpretation questions are common in many kinds of civil service tests. You are given a paragraph of written material and asked to find its central meaning.

3) Numerical ability

Number skills can be tested by the familiar arithmetic problem, by checking paired lists of numbers to see which are alike and which are different, or by interpreting charts and graphs. In the latter test, a graph may be printed in the test booklet which you are asked to use as the basis for answering questions.

4) Observation

A popular test for law-enforcement positions is the observation test. A picture is shown to you for several minutes, then taken away. Questions about the picture test your ability to observe both details and larger elements.

5) Following directions

In many positions in the public service, the employee must be able to carry out written instructions dependably and accurately. You may be given a chart with several columns, each column listing a variety of information. The questions require you to carry out directions involving the information given in the chart.

6) Skills and aptitudes

Performance tests effectively measure some manual skills and aptitudes. When the skill is one in which you are trained, such as typing or shorthand, you can practice. These tests are often very much like those given in business school or high school courses. For many of the other skills and aptitudes, however, no short-time preparation can be made. Skills and abilities natural to you or that you have developed throughout your lifetime are being tested.

Many of the general questions just described provide all the data needed to answer the questions and ask you to use your reasoning ability to find the answers. Your best preparation for these tests, as well as for tests of facts and ideas, is to be at your physical and mental best. You, no doubt, have your own methods of getting into an exam-taking mood and keeping "in shape." The next section lists some ideas on this subject.

IV. KINDS OF QUESTIONS

Only rarely is the "essay" question, which you answer in narrative form, used in civil service tests. Civil service tests are usually of the short-answer type. Full instructions for answering these questions will be given to you at the examination. But in case this is your first experience with short-answer questions and separate answer sheets, here is what you need to know:

1) Multiple-choice Questions

Most popular of the short-answer questions is the "multiple choice" or "best answer" question. It can be used, for example, to test for factual knowledge, ability to solve problems or judgment in meeting situations found at work.

A multiple-choice question is normally one of three types—
- It can begin with an incomplete statement followed by several possible endings. You are to find the one ending which *best* completes the statement, although some of the others may not be entirely wrong.
- It can also be a complete statement in the form of a question which is answered by choosing one of the statements listed.

- It can be in the form of a problem – again you select the best answer.

Here is an example of a multiple-choice question with a discussion which should give you some clues as to the method for choosing the right answer:

When an employee has a complaint about his assignment, the action which will *best* help him overcome his difficulty is to
- A. discuss his difficulty with his coworkers
- B. take the problem to the head of the organization
- C. take the problem to the person who gave him the assignment
- D. say nothing to anyone about his complaint

In answering this question, you should study each of the choices to find which is best. Consider choice "A" – Certainly an employee may discuss his complaint with fellow employees, but no change or improvement can result, and the complaint remains unresolved. Choice "B" is a poor choice since the head of the organization probably does not know what assignment you have been given, and taking your problem to him is known as "going over the head" of the supervisor. The supervisor, or person who made the assignment, is the person who can clarify it or correct any injustice. Choice "C" is, therefore, correct. To say nothing, as in choice "D," is unwise. Supervisors have and interest in knowing the problems employees are facing, and the employee is seeking a solution to his problem.

2) True/False Questions

The "true/false" or "right/wrong" form of question is sometimes used. Here a complete statement is given. Your job is to decide whether the statement is right or wrong.

SAMPLE: A roaming cell-phone call to a nearby city costs less than a non-roaming call to a distant city.

This statement is wrong, or false, since roaming calls are more expensive.

This is not a complete list of all possible question forms, although most of the others are variations of these common types. You will always get complete directions for answering questions. Be sure you understand *how* to mark your answers – ask questions until you do.

V. RECORDING YOUR ANSWERS

Computer terminals are used more and more today for many different kinds of exams.

For an examination with very few applicants, you may be told to record your answers in the test booklet itself. Separate answer sheets are much more common. If this separate answer sheet is to be scored by machine – and this is often the case – it is highly important that you mark your answers correctly in order to get credit.

An electronic scoring machine is often used in civil service offices because of the speed with which papers can be scored. Machine-scored answer sheets must be marked with a pencil, which will be given to you. This pencil has a high graphite content which responds to the electronic scoring machine. As a matter of fact, stray dots may register as answers, so do not let your pencil rest on the answer sheet while you are pondering the correct answer. Also, if your pencil lead breaks or is otherwise defective, ask for another.

Since the answer sheet will be dropped in a slot in the scoring machine, be careful not to bend the corners or get the paper crumpled.

The answer sheet normally has five vertical columns of numbers, with 30 numbers to a column. These numbers correspond to the question numbers in your test booklet. After each number, going across the page are four or five pairs of dotted lines. These short dotted lines have small letters or numbers above them. The first two pairs may also have a "T" or "F" above the letters. This indicates that the first two pairs only are to be used if the questions are of the true-false type. If the questions are multiple choice, disregard the "T" and "F" and pay attention only to the small letters or numbers.

Answer your questions in the manner of the sample that follows:

32. The largest city in the United States is
    A. Washington, D.C.
    B. New York City
    C. Chicago
    D. Detroit
    E. San Francisco

1) Choose the answer you think is best. (New York City is the largest, so "B" is correct.)
2) Find the row of dotted lines numbered the same as the question you are answering. (Find row number 32)
3) Find the pair of dotted lines corresponding to the answer. (Find the pair of lines under the mark "B.")
4) Make a solid black mark between the dotted lines.

VI. BEFORE THE TEST

Common sense will help you find procedures to follow to get ready for an examination. Too many of us, however, overlook these sensible measures. Indeed, nervousness and fatigue have been found to be the most serious reasons why applicants fail to do their best on civil service tests. Here is a list of reminders:

- Begin your preparation early – Don't wait until the last minute to go scurrying around for books and materials or to find out what the position is all about.
- Prepare continuously – An hour a night for a week is better than an all-night cram session. This has been definitely established. What is more, a night a week for a month will return better dividends than crowding your study into a shorter period of time.
- Locate the place of the exam – You have been sent a notice telling you when and where to report for the examination. If the location is in a different town or otherwise unfamiliar to you, it would be well to inquire the best route and learn something about the building.
- Relax the night before the test – Allow your mind to rest. Do not study at all that night. Plan some mild recreation or diversion; then go to bed early and get a good night's sleep.
- Get up early enough to make a leisurely trip to the place for the test – This way unforeseen events, traffic snarls, unfamiliar buildings, etc. will not upset you.
- Dress comfortably – A written test is not a fashion show. You will be known by number and not by name, so wear something comfortable.

- Leave excess paraphernalia at home – Shopping bags and odd bundles will get in your way. You need bring only the items mentioned in the official notice you received; usually everything you need is provided. Do not bring reference books to the exam. They will only confuse those last minutes and be taken away from you when in the test room.
- Arrive somewhat ahead of time – If because of transportation schedules you must get there very early, bring a newspaper or magazine to take your mind off yourself while waiting.
- Locate the examination room – When you have found the proper room, you will be directed to the seat or part of the room where you will sit. Sometimes you are given a sheet of instructions to read while you are waiting. Do not fill out any forms until you are told to do so; just read them and be prepared.
- Relax and prepare to listen to the instructions
- If you have any physical problem that may keep you from doing your best, be sure to tell the test administrator. If you are sick or in poor health, you really cannot do your best on the exam. You can come back and take the test some other time.

VII. AT THE TEST

The day of the test is here and you have the test booklet in your hand. The temptation to get going is very strong. Caution! There is more to success than knowing the right answers. You must know how to identify your papers and understand variations in the type of short-answer question used in this particular examination. Follow these suggestions for maximum results from your efforts:

1) Cooperate with the monitor

The test administrator has a duty to create a situation in which you can be as much at ease as possible. He will give instructions, tell you when to begin, check to see that you are marking your answer sheet correctly, and so on. He is not there to guard you, although he will see that your competitors do not take unfair advantage. He wants to help you do your best.

2) Listen to all instructions

Don't jump the gun! Wait until you understand all directions. In most civil service tests you get more time than you need to answer the questions. So don't be in a hurry. Read each word of instructions until you clearly understand the meaning. Study the examples, listen to all announcements and follow directions. Ask questions if you do not understand what to do.

3) Identify your papers

Civil service exams are usually identified by number only. You will be assigned a number; you must not put your name on your test papers. Be sure to copy your number correctly. Since more than one exam may be given, copy your exact examination title.

4) Plan your time

Unless you are told that a test is a "speed" or "rate of work" test, speed itself is usually not important. Time enough to answer all the questions will be provided, but this does not mean that you have all day. An overall time limit has been set. Divide the total time (in minutes) by the number of questions to determine the approximate time you have for each question.

5) Do not linger over difficult questions

If you come across a difficult question, mark it with a paper clip (useful to have along) and come back to it when you have been through the booklet. One caution if you do this – be sure to skip a number on your answer sheet as well. Check often to be sure that you have not lost your place and that you are marking in the row numbered the same as the question you are answering.

6) Read the questions

Be sure you know what the question asks! Many capable people are unsuccessful because they failed to *read* the questions correctly.

7) Answer all questions

Unless you have been instructed that a penalty will be deducted for incorrect answers, it is better to guess than to omit a question.

8) Speed tests

It is often better NOT to guess on speed tests. It has been found that on timed tests people are tempted to spend the last few seconds before time is called in marking answers at random – without even reading them – in the hope of picking up a few extra points. To discourage this practice, the instructions may warn you that your score will be "corrected" for guessing. That is, a penalty will be applied. The incorrect answers will be deducted from the correct ones, or some other penalty formula will be used.

9) Review your answers

If you finish before time is called, go back to the questions you guessed or omitted to give them further thought. Review other answers if you have time.

10) Return your test materials

If you are ready to leave before others have finished or time is called, take ALL your materials to the monitor and leave quietly. Never take any test material with you. The monitor can discover whose papers are not complete, and taking a test booklet may be grounds for disqualification.

VIII. EXAMINATION TECHNIQUES

1) Read the general instructions carefully. These are usually printed on the first page of the exam booklet. As a rule, these instructions refer to the timing of the examination; the fact that you should not start work until the signal and must stop work at a signal, etc. If there are any *special* instructions, such as a choice of questions to be answered, make sure that you note this instruction carefully.

2) When you are ready to start work on the examination, that is as soon as the signal has been given, read the instructions to each question booklet, underline any key words or phrases, such as *least, best, outline, describe* and the like. In this way you will tend to answer as requested rather than discover on reviewing your paper that you *listed without describing*, that you selected the *worst* choice rather than the *best* choice, etc.

3) If the examination is of the objective or multiple-choice type – that is, each question will also give a series of possible answers: A, B, C or D, and you are called upon to select the best answer and write the letter next to that answer on your answer paper – it is advisable to start answering each question in turn. There may be anywhere from 50 to 100 such questions in the three or four hours allotted and you can see how much time would be taken if you read through all the questions before beginning to answer any. Furthermore, if you come across a question or group of questions which you know would be difficult to answer, it would undoubtedly affect your handling of all the other questions.

4) If the examination is of the essay type and contains but a few questions, it is a moot point as to whether you should read all the questions before starting to answer any one. Of course, if you are given a choice – say five out of seven and the like – then it is essential to read all the questions so you can eliminate the two that are most difficult. If, however, you are asked to answer all the questions, there may be danger in trying to answer the easiest one first because you may find that you will spend too much time on it. The best technique is to answer the first question, then proceed to the second, etc.

5) Time your answers. Before the exam begins, write down the time it started, then add the time allowed for the examination and write down the time it must be completed, then divide the time available somewhat as follows:
    - If 3-1/2 hours are allowed, that would be 210 minutes. If you have 80 objective-type questions, that would be an average of 2-1/2 minutes per question. Allow yourself no more than 2 minutes per question, or a total of 160 minutes, which will permit about 50 minutes to review.
    - If for the time allotment of 210 minutes there are 7 essay questions to answer, that would average about 30 minutes a question. Give yourself only 25 minutes per question so that you have about 35 minutes to review.

6) The most important instruction is to *read each question* and make sure you know what is wanted. The second most important instruction is to *time yourself properly* so that you answer every question. The third most important instruction is to *answer every question*. Guess if you have to but include something for each question. Remember that you will receive no credit for a blank and will probably receive some credit if you write something in answer to an essay question. If you guess a letter – say "B" for a multiple-choice question – you may have guessed right. If you leave a blank as an answer to a multiple-choice question, the examiners may respect your feelings but it will not add a point to your score. Some exams may penalize you for wrong answers, so in such cases *only*, you may not want to guess unless you have some basis for your answer.

7) Suggestions
    a. Objective-type questions
        1. Examine the question booklet for proper sequence of pages and questions
        2. Read all instructions carefully
        3. Skip any question which seems too difficult; return to it after all other questions have been answered
        4. Apportion your time properly; do not spend too much time on any single question or group of questions

5. Note and underline key words – *all, most, fewest, least, best, worst, same, opposite,* etc.
6. Pay particular attention to negatives
7. Note unusual option, e.g., unduly long, short, complex, different or similar in content to the body of the question
8. Observe the use of "hedging" words – *probably, may, most likely,* etc.
9. Make sure that your answer is put next to the same number as the question
10. Do not second-guess unless you have good reason to believe the second answer is definitely more correct
11. Cross out original answer if you decide another answer is more accurate; do not erase until you are ready to hand your paper in
12. Answer all questions; guess unless instructed otherwise
13. Leave time for review

b. Essay questions
   1. Read each question carefully
   2. Determine exactly what is wanted. Underline key words or phrases.
   3. Decide on outline or paragraph answer
   4. Include many different points and elements unless asked to develop any one or two points or elements
   5. Show impartiality by giving pros and cons unless directed to select one side only
   6. Make and write down any assumptions you find necessary to answer the questions
   7. Watch your English, grammar, punctuation and choice of words
   8. Time your answers; don't crowd material

8) Answering the essay question

Most essay questions can be answered by framing the specific response around several key words or ideas. Here are a few such key words or ideas:

M's: manpower, materials, methods, money, management
P's: purpose, program, policy, plan, procedure, practice, problems, pitfalls, personnel, public relations

   a. Six basic steps in handling problems:
      1. Preliminary plan and background development
      2. Collect information, data and facts
      3. Analyze and interpret information, data and facts
      4. Analyze and develop solutions as well as make recommendations
      5. Prepare report and sell recommendations
      6. Install recommendations and follow up effectiveness

   b. Pitfalls to avoid
      1. *Taking things for granted* – A statement of the situation does not necessarily imply that each of the elements is necessarily true; for example, a complaint may be invalid and biased so that all that can be taken for granted is that a complaint has been registered

2. *Considering only one side of a situation* – Wherever possible, indicate several alternatives and then point out the reasons you selected the best one
3. *Failing to indicate follow up* – Whenever your answer indicates action on your part, make certain that you will take proper follow-up action to see how successful your recommendations, procedures or actions turn out to be
4. *Taking too long in answering any single question* – Remember to time your answers properly

IX. AFTER THE TEST

Scoring procedures differ in detail among civil service jurisdictions although the general principles are the same. Whether the papers are hand-scored or graded by machine we have described, they are nearly always graded by number. That is, the person who marks the paper knows only the number – never the name – of the applicant. Not until all the papers have been graded will they be matched with names. If other tests, such as training and experience or oral interview ratings have been given, scores will be combined. Different parts of the examination usually have different weights. For example, the written test might count 60 percent of the final grade, and a rating of training and experience 40 percent. In many jurisdictions, veterans will have a certain number of points added to their grades.

After the final grade has been determined, the names are placed in grade order and an eligible list is established. There are various methods for resolving ties between those who get the same final grade – probably the most common is to place first the name of the person whose application was received first. Job offers are made from the eligible list in the order the names appear on it. You will be notified of your grade and your rank as soon as all these computations have been made. This will be done as rapidly as possible.

People who are found to meet the requirements in the announcement are called "eligibles." Their names are put on a list of eligible candidates. An eligible's chances of getting a job depend on how high he stands on this list and how fast agencies are filling jobs from the list.

When a job is to be filled from a list of eligibles, the agency asks for the names of people on the list of eligibles for that job. When the civil service commission receives this request, it sends to the agency the names of the three people highest on this list. Or, if the job to be filled has specialized requirements, the office sends the agency the names of the top three persons who meet these requirements from the general list.

The appointing officer makes a choice from among the three people whose names were sent to him. If the selected person accepts the appointment, the names of the others are put back on the list to be considered for future openings.

That is the rule in hiring from all kinds of eligible lists, whether they are for typist, carpenter, chemist, or something else. For every vacancy, the appointing officer has his choice of any one of the top three eligibles on the list. This explains why the person whose name is on top of the list sometimes does not get an appointment when some of the persons lower on the list do. If the appointing officer chooses the second or third eligible, the No. 1 eligible does not get a job at once, but stays on the list until he is appointed or the list is terminated.

X. HOW TO PASS THE INTERVIEW TEST

The examination for which you applied requires an oral interview test. You have already taken the written test and you are now being called for the interview test – the final part of the formal examination.

You may think that it is not possible to prepare for an interview test and that there are no procedures to follow during an interview. Our purpose is to point out some things you can do in advance that will help you and some good rules to follow and pitfalls to avoid while you are being interviewed.

What is an interview supposed to test?

The written examination is designed to test the technical knowledge and competence of the candidate; the oral is designed to evaluate intangible qualities, not readily measured otherwise, and to establish a list showing the relative fitness of each candidate – as measured against his competitors – for the position sought. Scoring is not on the basis of "right" and "wrong," but on a sliding scale of values ranging from "not passable" to "outstanding." As a matter of fact, it is possible to achieve a relatively low score without a single "incorrect" answer because of evident weakness in the qualities being measured.

Occasionally, an examination may consist entirely of an oral test – either an individual or a group oral. In such cases, information is sought concerning the technical knowledges and abilities of the candidate, since there has been no written examination for this purpose. More commonly, however, an oral test is used to supplement a written examination.

Who conducts interviews?

The composition of oral boards varies among different jurisdictions. In nearly all, a representative of the personnel department serves as chairman. One of the members of the board may be a representative of the department in which the candidate would work. In some cases, "outside experts" are used, and, frequently, a businessman or some other representative of the general public is asked to serve. Labor and management or other special groups may be represented. The aim is to secure the services of experts in the appropriate field.

However the board is composed, it is a good idea (and not at all improper or unethical) to ascertain in advance of the interview who the members are and what groups they represent. When you are introduced to them, you will have some idea of their backgrounds and interests, and at least you will not stutter and stammer over their names.

What should be done before the interview?

While knowledge about the board members is useful and takes some of the surprise element out of the interview, there is other preparation which is more substantive. It *is* possible to prepare for an oral interview – in several ways:

1) Keep a copy of your application and review it carefully before the interview

This may be the only document before the oral board, and the starting point of the interview. Know what education and experience you have listed there, and the sequence and dates of all of it. Sometimes the board will ask you to review the highlights of your experience for them; you should not have to hem and haw doing it.

2) Study the class specification and the examination announcement

Usually, the oral board has one or both of these to guide them. The qualities, characteristics or knowledges required by the position sought are stated in these documents. They offer valuable clues as to the nature of the oral interview. For example, if the job involves supervisory responsibilities, the announcement will usually indicate that knowledge of modern supervisory methods and the qualifications of the candidate as a supervisor will be tested. If so, you can expect such questions, frequently in the form of a hypothetical situation which you are expected to solve. NEVER go into an oral without knowledge of the duties and responsibilities of the job you seek.

3) Think through each qualification required

Try to visualize the kind of questions you would ask if you were a board member. How well could you answer them? Try especially to appraise your own knowledge and background in each area, *measured against the job sought*, and identify any areas in which you are weak. Be critical and realistic – do not flatter yourself.

4) Do some general reading in areas in which you feel you may be weak

For example, if the job involves supervision and your past experience has NOT, some general reading in supervisory methods and practices, particularly in the field of human relations, might be useful. Do NOT study agency procedures or detailed manuals. The oral board will be testing your understanding and capacity, not your memory.

5) Get a good night's sleep and watch your general health and mental attitude

You will want a clear head at the interview. Take care of a cold or any other minor ailment, and of course, no hangovers.

What should be done on the day of the interview?

Now comes the day of the interview itself. Give yourself plenty of time to get there. Plan to arrive somewhat ahead of the scheduled time, particularly if your appointment is in the fore part of the day. If a previous candidate fails to appear, the board might be ready for you a bit early. By early afternoon an oral board is almost invariably behind schedule if there are many candidates, and you may have to wait. Take along a book or magazine to read, or your application to review, but leave any extraneous material in the waiting room when you go in for your interview. In any event, relax and compose yourself.

The matter of dress is important. The board is forming impressions about you – from your experience, your manners, your attitude, and your appearance. Give your personal appearance careful attention. Dress your best, but not your flashiest. Choose conservative, appropriate clothing, and be sure it is immaculate. This is a business interview, and your appearance should indicate that you regard it as such. Besides, being well groomed and properly dressed will help boost your confidence.

Sooner or later, someone will call your name and escort you into the interview room. *This is it.* From here on you are on your own. It is too late for any more preparation. But remember, you asked for this opportunity to prove your fitness, and you are here because your request was granted.

What happens when you go in?

The usual sequence of events will be as follows: The clerk (who is often the board stenographer) will introduce you to the chairman of the oral board, who will introduce you to the other members of the board. Acknowledge the introductions before you sit down. Do not be surprised if you find a microphone facing you or a stenotypist sitting by. Oral interviews are usually recorded in the event of an appeal or other review.

Usually the chairman of the board will open the interview by reviewing the highlights of your education and work experience from your application – primarily for the benefit of the other members of the board, as well as to get the material into the record. Do not interrupt or comment unless there is an error or significant misinterpretation; if that is the case, do not hesitate. But do not quibble about insignificant matters. Also, he will usually ask you some question about your education, experience or your present job – partly to get you to start talking and to establish the interviewing "rapport." He may start the actual questioning, or turn it over to one of the other members. Frequently, each member undertakes the questioning on a particular area, one in which he is perhaps most competent, so you can expect each member to participate in the examination. Because time is limited, you may also expect some rather abrupt switches in the direction the questioning takes, so do not be upset by it. Normally, a board member will not pursue a single line of questioning unless he discovers a particular strength or weakness.

After each member has participated, the chairman will usually ask whether any member has any further questions, then will ask you if you have anything you wish to add. Unless you are expecting this question, it may floor you. Worse, it may start you off on an extended, extemporaneous speech. The board is not usually seeking more information. The question is principally to offer you a last opportunity to present further qualifications or to indicate that you have nothing to add. So, if you feel that a significant qualification or characteristic has been overlooked, it is proper to point it out in a sentence or so. Do not compliment the board on the thoroughness of their examination – they have been sketchy, and you know it. If you wish, merely say, "No thank you, I have nothing further to add." This is a point where you can "talk yourself out" of a good impression or fail to present an important bit of information. Remember, *you close the interview yourself.*

The chairman will then say, "That is all, Mr. _____, thank you." Do not be startled; the interview is over, and quicker than you think. Thank him, gather your belongings and take your leave. Save your sigh of relief for the other side of the door.

How to put your best foot forward

Throughout this entire process, you may feel that the board individually and collectively is trying to pierce your defenses, seek out your hidden weaknesses and embarrass and confuse you. Actually, this is not true. They are obliged to make an appraisal of your qualifications for the job you are seeking, and they want to see you in your best light. Remember, they must interview all candidates and a non-cooperative candidate may become a failure in spite of their best efforts to bring out his qualifications. Here are 15 suggestions that will help you:

1) **Be natural – Keep your attitude confident, not cocky**

If you are not confident that you can do the job, do not expect the board to be. Do not apologize for your weaknesses, try to bring out your strong points. The board is interested in a positive, not negative, presentation. Cockiness will antagonize any board member and make him wonder if you are covering up a weakness by a false show of strength.

2) **Get comfortable, but don't lounge or sprawl**

Sit erectly but not stiffly. A careless posture may lead the board to conclude that you are careless in other things, or at least that you are not impressed by the importance of the occasion. Either conclusion is natural, even if incorrect. Do not fuss with your clothing, a pencil or an ashtray. Your hands may occasionally be useful to emphasize a point; do not let them become a point of distraction.

3) **Do not wisecrack or make small talk**

This is a serious situation, and your attitude should show that you consider it as such. Further, the time of the board is limited – they do not want to waste it, and neither should you.

4) Do not exaggerate your experience or abilities

In the first place, from information in the application or other interviews and sources, the board may know more about you than you think. Secondly, you probably will not get away with it. An experienced board is rather adept at spotting such a situation, so do not take the chance.

5) If you know a board member, do not make a point of it, yet do not hide it

Certainly you are not fooling him, and probably not the other members of the board. Do not try to take advantage of your acquaintanceship – it will probably do you little good.

6) Do not dominate the interview

Let the board do that. They will give you the clues – do not assume that you have to do all the talking. Realize that the board has a number of questions to ask you, and do not try to take up all the interview time by showing off your extensive knowledge of the answer to the first one.

7) Be attentive

You only have 20 minutes or so, and you should keep your attention at its sharpest throughout. When a member is addressing a problem or question to you, give him your undivided attention. Address your reply principally to him, but do not exclude the other board members.

8) Do not interrupt

A board member may be stating a problem for you to analyze. He will ask you a question when the time comes. Let him state the problem, and wait for the question.

9) Make sure you understand the question

Do not try to answer until you are sure what the question is. If it is not clear, restate it in your own words or ask the board member to clarify it for you. However, do not haggle about minor elements.

10) Reply promptly but not hastily

A common entry on oral board rating sheets is "candidate responded readily," or "candidate hesitated in replies." Respond as promptly and quickly as you can, but do not jump to a hasty, ill-considered answer.

11) Do not be peremptory in your answers

A brief answer is proper – but do not fire your answer back. That is a losing game from your point of view. The board member can probably ask questions much faster than you can answer them.

12) Do not try to create the answer you think the board member wants

He is interested in what kind of mind you have and how it works – not in playing games. Furthermore, he can usually spot this practice and will actually grade you down on it.

13) Do not switch sides in your reply merely to agree with a board member

Frequently, a member will take a contrary position merely to draw you out and to see if you are willing and able to defend your point of view. Do not start a debate, yet do not surrender a good position. If a position is worth taking, it is worth defending.

14) Do not be afraid to admit an error in judgment if you are shown to be wrong

The board knows that you are forced to reply without any opportunity for careful consideration. Your answer may be demonstrably wrong. If so, admit it and get on with the interview.

15) Do not dwell at length on your present job

The opening question may relate to your present assignment. Answer the question but do not go into an extended discussion. You are being examined for a *new* job, not your present one. As a matter of fact, try to phrase ALL your answers in terms of the job for which you are being examined.

Basis of Rating

Probably you will forget most of these "do's" and "don'ts" when you walk into the oral interview room. Even remembering them all will not ensure you a passing grade. Perhaps you did not have the qualifications in the first place. But remembering them will help you to put your best foot forward, without treading on the toes of the board members.

Rumor and popular opinion to the contrary notwithstanding, an oral board wants you to make the best appearance possible. They know you are under pressure – but they also want to see how you respond to it as a guide to what your reaction would be under the pressures of the job you seek. They will be influenced by the degree of poise you display, the personal traits you show and the manner in which you respond.

ABOUT THIS BOOK

This book contains tests divided into Examination Sections. Go through each test, answering every question in the margin. We have also attached a sample answer sheet at the back of the book that can be removed and used. At the end of each test look at the answer key and check your answers. On the ones you got wrong, look at the right answer choice and learn. Do not fill in the answers first. Do not memorize the questions and answers, but understand the answer and principles involved. On your test, the questions will likely be different from the samples. Questions are changed and new ones added. If you understand these past questions you should have success with any changes that arise. Tests may consist of several types of questions. We have additional books on each subject should more study be advisable or necessary for you. Finally, the more you study, the better prepared you will be. This book is intended to be the last thing you study before you walk into the examination room. Prior study of relevant texts is also recommended. NLC publishes some of these in our Fundamental Series. Knowledge and good sense are important factors in passing your exam. Good luck also helps. So now study this Passbook, absorb the material contained within and take that knowledge into the examination. Then do your best to pass that exam.

EXAMINATION SECTION

EXAMINATION SECTION
TEST 1

DIRECTIONS: Each question or incomplete statement is followed by several suggested answers or completions. Select the one that BEST answers the question or completes the statement. *PRINT THE LETTER OF THE CORRECT ANSWER IN THE SPACE AT THE RIGHT.*

1. An Assistant Housing Manager has called a subordinate into his office in order to discuss the subordinate's failure to perform some task adequately. The subordinate, when criticized, accused the Assistant Manager of being prejudiced against him. If this is the first time that such an incident has occurred, it would be best for the manager to

    A. assure the subordinate that the facts upon which the criticism was based will be reviewed, since the subordinate feels so strongly about the matter
    B. insist that the subordinate listen to the criticism and that he make no comment on it unless he can do so in an objective manner
    C. listen to whatever the subordinate has to say and indicate the basis for the criticism
    D. terminate the interview immediately and suggest that the discussion be continued at some other time

2. Faced with a subordinate who is excessively dependent upon his superior in arriving at decisions, the superior should

    A. arrange to have the subordinate transferred to work which will not involve decision making
    B. continue to assist him in making decisions while instilling a feeling of confidence in the subordinate
    C. direct the subordinate to make his own decisions in areas assigned to him
    D. reprimand the subordinate for failing to perform the job properly

3. A supervisor has called one of his subordinates into his office to inform him of his service rating. During the interview, the supervisor has praised the subordinate for his good points and also criticized his shortcomings. The subordinate has agreed without discussion to every criticism leveled against him by the supervisor. It would now be best for the supervisor to

    A. get the employee to review his shortcomings and to suggest a plan for minimizing them, before terminating the interview
    B. suggest that the employee reserve any opinion on the criticisms until the service rating appeal period
    C. terminate the interview after having outlined all of the employee's shortcomings and points of merit
    D. terminate the interview after praising the employee's general receptiveness to criticism and emphasizing that past mistakes will not count against him in the coming year

4. A report to be sent to another subdivision of the Housing Authority has been prepared by a competent subordinate, in the name of the supervisor. It would be best for the supervisor to

   A. check the report in detail since it bears his name
   B. have the report checked in detail by another competent subordinate
   C. review the report briefly to pick up any obvious errors or omissions
   D. send the report forward without reading it

4.____

5. In establishing a work schedule for the performance of a particular job, the one of the following which is of LEAST importance is the

   A. number of employees available for assignment
   B. time by which the job must be finished
   C. time required for each separate part of the total job
   D. time required under very difficult or adverse conditions

5.____

6. One of the chief responsibilities of the supervisor is to make sure that the work is completed on time. In order to achieve this aim, it would be desirable for the supervisor to

   A. assign one employee to each specific task
   B. delegate responsibility in accordance with the abilities and capacities of his subordinates
   C. help out by doing as much of the work himself as he can
   D. schedule the work and keep informed of its progress

6.____

7. Effective supervisors apply proper principles of human relations. Application of such principles has what kind of effect on the need for detailed rules and regulations covering every aspect of the job?

   A. has no effect upon it
   B. increases the need for it
   C. reduces the need for it
   D. supersedes rules and regulations

7.____

8. Of the following, the most important generally approved method of maintaining high morale in one's staff is to

   A. advise the staff that personal problems must be left at home
   B. employ a jocular manner in issuing such reprimands as are necessary
   C. keep the staff informed of new developments and policies of the Housing Authority
   D. praise employees whenever such praise is warranted and refrain from direct criticism of their faults

8.____

9. When you become aware that a Housing Assistant under your supervision has failed to follow the proper procedure in making apartment inspections and has concealed this failure, it would be best for you to

   A. discuss with him both the failure to follow the proper procedure and the reason for this concealment, with the aim of improving the relationship between superior and subordinate
   B. make no mention of the matter to the assistant, but watch him more closely in the future

9.____

C. inform the assistant that the proper apartment inspection procedure must be followed since a uniform procedure is necessary for effective project management
D. review the proper apartment inspection procedure with the assistant and reprimand him for having concealed his failure to follow it

10. "The project manager does not formulate Housing Authority policy, but is responsible for executing policy formulated by top management. He is the administrative person closest to the employee group carrying out actual operations."
On this basis, a chLief function of the manager is to

   A. dissuade employees from giving suggestions on translating policy into action
   B. interpret policy in a way which will respect the personal interests and needs of the employees
   C. recommend promotion of personnel to top management
   D. report work schedules, work delays and staff assignments to top management so all the facts are available for decision making

11. The one of the following which is NOT a principle of effective operation in an organization is the need to

   A. coordinate the work of different divisions
   B. delegate to subordinates as much authority as they can assume within the scope of their jobs
   C. provide sufficient overlapping of authority to insure coverage of all aspects of operation
   D. trace and isolate problems, obstructions and other difficulties

12. A supervisor is most likely to achieve increased production by setting

   A. high but attainable goals, and according high praise to those subordinates who reach the goals
   B. low goals, and according high praise to those subordinates who exceed the goals
   C. moderately high goals, raising them as the more efficient subordinates approach them
   D. very high goals, and pressing the subordinates to reach them

13. Of the following, the most practical method of acquainting new employees with the details of routine rules and regulations of the Housing Authority is to

   A. assign each new employee to an older employee for instruction and clarification of procedures
   B. discuss with each new employee the nature of such rules and regulations shortly after he begins work
   C. hold a conference with all new employees to inform them of the rules and regulations
   D. provide a manual of rules and regulations for each employee

14. The practice of supervisors making themselves available to subordinates in order to listen to and help solve the subordinates' personal (off the job) problems is regarded as

    A. a form of paternalism rejected by both management and labor
    B. inadvisable since supervisors are seldom equipped to do such counseling
    C. proper in the maintenance of good personal relations
    D. undesirable since it represents the intrusion into the subordinates' personal affairs

15. An important educational principle that should be recognized by supervisors who are training subordinates is that

    A. any effective method of instruction will work equally well with all subordinates in a given title
    B. individual instruction is the only reliable method of training the average individual
    C. interested and capable persons will learn at different rates of speed when taking the same course of training
    D. people over 60 years of age have little capacity for learning

16. Assume that a Housing Manager disagrees with a new policy which has just been adopted by the central office. When he explains to his staff the policy and its application, there are criticisms and objections, many of which reflect his own point of view. It would be best for the manager to

    A. agree that the policy is defective but direct that it must be carried out
    B. explain the basis for the policy and order the staff to follow it
    C. modify the policy to meet the most valid objections to insure willing compliance with the policy
    D. refute the criticisms and objections regardless of his own opinion in the matter

17. A staff conference has been called by a supervisor for the purpose of considering means which may be used to solve a particular problem. In this situation, it is most important for the supervisor to

    A. encourage discussion, but discourage argument
    B. express his own views and opinions first
    C. permit the discussion to continue until everyone attending the conference is satisfied he has had his full say
    D. remain impartial, indicating neither approval or disapproval of any suggestions which may be presented

18. At staff meetings a manager is faced with a subordinate who takes every opportunity to make comments and gripe about one particular procedure. It would be best for the manager to

    A. assert his authority and warn the griper that publicly aired complaints will not be tolerated
    B. briefly explain management's reason for the procedure griped about
    C. ignore the gripes
    D. tell the griper that the problem at hand is how best to operate under the established procedure

19. One member of the staff, at staff meetings, likes to argue frequently and at length. It would be best for the supervisor to

   A. exclude him from staff meetings
   B. hear his arguments and answer them briefly
   C. talk to him privately and enlist his help in reducing arguments at staff meetings
   D. talk to other members of the staff, requesting that they not become involved in arguments with the offending member

20. At a staff conference conducted by you, there are frequent interruptions of the general discussion which indicate lack of understanding of the objectives of the conference. Of the following, the most reasonable conclusion to draw from this situation is that

   A. adequate control over the trend of the discussion was lacking
   B. conferees were probably antagonistic to the objectives of the conference
   C. content of the discussion bore little relation to the actual work assignments of the conferees
   D. objectives of the conference may not have been clearly expressed at the start of the conference

21. One of the staff members at a project frequently has good ideas but expresses them poorly when presenting them at staff meetings. It would be best for the manager to

   A. accept the ideas as they are presented, without commenting on the method of expression
   B. allow the staff member to state his ideas and for the manager to paraphrase them so they are easily understood
   C. defer consideration of the ideas until the next staff meeting so that the staff member can have time to put them in clearer form
   D. suggest to the staff member that he inform the manager of his ideas before the meeting so that the manager can rephrase them and present them so that they are more easily understood

22. In the course of several interviews with a certain tenant, you notice several incidents of peculiar behavior on the part of her child whom she has brought along with her to the office. The behavior appears to indicate an emotional disturbance requiring psychiatric help. The most advisable course of action for you to follow is to

   A. bring the situation to the attention of a child guidance clinic so that they may take appropriate action
   B. discuss the situation with the mother in an attempt to make her aware of the problem and the possible need for treatment
   C. tactfully point out to the mother that the child is emotionally disturbed and should be treated by a psychiatrist
   D. take no action on the situation but make a note of it in the tenant folder

23. An accepted concept of management of public housing is that it should "studiously avoid attitudes of paternalism." To avoid the paternalistic approach in dealing with tenants, management should

   A. deal with tenants as individuals rather than in organized groups
   B. emphasize its interest in good tenant relations, but avoid making specific recommendations on problems brought to it by tenants

C. emphasize objective uniform procedures in dealing with tenant problems
D. not interest itself in an unemployment problem brought to its attention by a tenant

24. Housing management should realize that the most essential factor contributing to the success of a community activities program is

   A. adequacy of facilities
   B. availability of funds
   C. existence of a sponsoring agency
   D. quality of leadership in activities

25. The one of the following which LEAST characterizes the dealings of the Housing Authority with agencies sponsoring community activities programs in projects is that the Authority

   A. gives certain forms of financial assistance
   B. permits retention of agency identity
   C. provides government direction
   D. requires reports on activities and progress

KEY (CORRECT ANSWERS)

1. C	11. C
2. B	12. A
3. A	13. D
4. C	14. C
5. D	15. C
6. D	16. B
7. C	17. A
8. C	18. D
9. A	19. C
10. B	20. D

21. B
22. B
23. C
24. D
25. C

TEST 2

DIRECTIONS: Each question or incomplete statement is followed by several suggested answers or completions. Select the one that BEST answers the question or completes the statement. *PRINT THE LETTER OF THE CORRECT ANSWER IN THE SPACE AT THE RIGHT.*

1. The one of the following which best indicates the extent to which teenage boys and girls may be permitted to plan their own leisure-time activities program is:

    A. Give the teenagers full responsibility for planning
    B. Leave the planning in the hands of the community activities coordinator or other professional leadership
    C. Permit certain selected teenagers to offer suggestions on planning, but leave all decisions up to the community activities coordinator
    D. Provide for joint responsibility of teenagers and professional leadership in planning

2. A frequent criticism of the construction of public housing developments in slum areas has been the

    A. failure to consider the transportation needs of tenants
    B. failure to modify in any way the established gridiron pattern of slum thoroughfares
    C. failure to reduce population densities to desirable density standards
    D. lack of provision for slum site families in public housing developments

3. As part of a report to the central office, a graph is to be prepared to show the rental income of a housing project, the amount which has been spent on heating, and the amount which has been spent on maintenance, each year for a five-year period. The best type of graph to use is a

    A. bar graph
    B. circle graph
    C. pictorial graph
    D. proportional graph

4. Of the following arguments which may be used in an effort to urge residential site tenants to move, the LEAST suitable is to

    A. assure displaced families that they will be given first preference in choice of apartments in the new project
    B. explain that new projects will provide wholesome housing quarters for many families
    C. indicate why a slum area is not a desirable place in which to live and raise a family
    D. point out that stores, movies and other similar services will soon go out of business to make room for the new project

5. The Housing Authority does not usually attempt to replace or make major improvements in the heating and plumbing systems of site buildings, even when such systems are somewhat defective or present operating difficulties. The chief reason for this policy is that

    A. buildings on sites are of such a heterogeneous nature and generally so out-of-date that repair and replacement parts are unobtainable
    B. it is economically unsound to make major improvements in buildings which will soon be demolished

C. poor heating and plumbing services are very effective in encouraging tenants to move as quickly as possible
D. there is no need for the Authority to make repairs which the previous owner was unwilling to make

6. A site building has a coal-fired steam boiler as the heating plant. While using the boiler, proper examination of the water gauge fails to reveal the presence of any water. Of the following, it would be best that

    A. a small amount of water be let into the boiler immediately, increasing the amount of water gradually until the proper level is reached
    B. the fire be put out immediately by covering with sand
    C. the fire be put out immediately by spraying with warm water
    D. the required amount of water be put into the boiler immediately

7. The principal reason why a record is kept of "removable items" (so designated by the city's appraisers) which are left behind by commercial site tenants when they move out is that the

    A. award for moving expenses may be appropriately reduced
    B. commercial tenant may receive an award for the removable items
    C. items may be enumerated and taken into account in demolition contracts
    D. presence of the items will be known in the event they are reclassified as fixtures

8. When a commercial tenant, occupying space in a building purchased by the Housing Authority for demolition, moves prior to the date of condemnation, leaving behind certain fixtures, he is ordinarily entitled to

    A. a fixture award plus moving expenses
    B. a fixture award to be paid by the former owner as determined by the court at the time of condemnation
    C. no fixture award
    D. the same fixture award he would receive if he had waited until after the date of condemnation

9. To expedite the clearance of one site it may be necessary to transfer a residential tenant to a second site. In this event, the tenant is entitled, in so far as priority for admission to a project is concerned, to

    A. former site occupant status at the first site but no preference at the second site
    B. no former site occupant status but preference for admission to a project so long as he remains a site tenant
    C. site occupant status at the second site but no preference at the first site
    D. site tenant status at the second site and former site occupant status at the first site

10. Security deposits are required of all project tenants EXCEPT the following:

    A. recipients of assistance from the Department of Welfare
    B. resident employees
    C. resident employees and recipients of full assistance from the Department of Welfare
    D. resident employees and recipients of full Old Age Assistance

11. The most accurate statement concerning the eligibility for public housing of persons engaged in professional occupations, such as doctors, dentists or lawyers, is that they are

    A. eligible on the same basis as non-professionals
    B. eligible when engaged in their profession only part time, and if they meet the standards of eligibility, including income
    C. eligible when not self-employed, and if they meet the standards of eligibility, including income
    D. ineligible under all circumstances

11._____

12. A family group consisting of a husband, wife, son and an unrelated individual who has resided with them for 20 years applies for a project apartment. Considering family composition only, this family group is

    A. eligible for admission only to federally aided and city-aided projects
    B. eligible for admission only to state-aided and city-aided projects
    C. eligible for admission to all projects
    D. not eligible for public housing

12._____

13. A natural family group contains, in addition, one or more foster children for the support of whom the family receives remuneration from an accredited social agency. If the family meets other eligibility requirements, it is eligible for admission to

    A. all projects, the remuneration not to be considered income
    B. all projects, the remuneration not to be considered in determining eligibility, but to be considered in determining rent
    C. all projects, but, in the case of federally aided projects, the remuneration is to be considered income in determining rent and eligibility
    D. federally and city-aided projects only

13._____

14. The one of the following which is the most complete list of requirements for eligibility for an apartment in a public housing project for a single-person family is:

    A. 55 years of age or older; has been maintaining his own separate living quarters, or is a roomer in a hotel, rooming house or lodging house
    B. physically able to care for himself; able to maintain his apartment; 55 years of age or older; has been maintaining his own separate living quarters
    C. physically able to care for himself; 50 years of age or older; has been maintaining his own separate living quarters, or is a roomer in a hotel, rooming house or lodging house
    D. physically able to care for himself; 50 years of age or older

14._____

15. If a tenant who has been served with a notice of ineligibility, but not with a notice to vacate, moves from his apartment without notifying the Housing Authority prior to the date of move-out, he shall be charged rent

    A. for a period not to exceed seven days after the date of move-out, depending on the vacancy loss
    B. for a period not to exceed 15 days after the date of move-out, depending on the vacancy loss
    C. only through the date of move-out
    D. for the full calendar month, regardless of vacancy loss

15._____

16. As the population of cities increases, there is a decrease in the proportion of the developed urban land area which is used for

    A. commercial purposes
    B. industrial purposes
    C. parks and open areas
    D. residential purposes
    E. streets and thoroughfares

17. If valid criteria have been used in tenant selection for public housing projects, the result most likely to be attained is

    A. homogeneity of tenant characteristics will be assured
    B. larger Federal subsidies will be required
    C. neediest families will receive the greatest proportion of aid
    D. the underlying conditions of slums will be ameliorated
    E. management problems will be satisfied

18. On August 26 a tenant notifies the project of an increase in income which became effective on August 12. This increased income will require a rent increase for the tenant. His new increased rent becomes effective on the first of

    A. August   B. September   C. October   D. November

19. In calculating the anticipated income of a project tenant, the one of the following which shall NOT be included is

    A. unemployment insurance benefits
    B. veteran's mustering-out payments
    C. Workmen's Compensation payments
    D. Workmen's Compensation payments, when the employee also has income from other employment

20. An investigation has been made of a broken window pane in an apartment on the third floor which the tenant claims was broken by children playing outside. The investigation disclosed that there were several small holes in the window pane. Each hole is approximately cone-shaped and is about 3/16 inch in diameter on the inside of the glass (room side) and about 1/2 inch in diameter on the outside. Cracks connected some of these holes. On the basis of this information, the tenant should

    A. be charged for the window pane since the damage is not normal wear-and-tear and it is not possible to substantiate the tenant's claim
    B. be charged for the window pane since the nature of the damage indicates that it was caused from inside
    C. not be charged for the window pane since it is not possible to determine the cause of the damage and the low floor involved does not tend to support the tenant's explanation
    D. not be charged for the window pane since the nature of the damage indicates that it was caused from outside

21. Suppose you are studying the need for improving the effectiveness of operation of a particular activity. In making this study, you should pay LEAST attention to the   21.____

    A. amount of time which is consumed in this activity
    B. degree of prestige which will accrue to you
    C. number of persons engaged in this activity
    D. possible revision of employee work schedules
    E. value of the end product resulting from the activity

22. In training employees under your supervision, a basic fact to recognize is that   22.____

    A. instruction should be the same for all, since learning rates are uniform for all employees in a given title
    B. it is difficult to train persons above the age of 40 years
    C. persons differ in the amount they learn in a given period of time
    D. the training process should begin on a highly technical level if the subject matter to be learned is highly technical
    E. training can seldom achieve its purpose unless individual instruction is the method used

23. A group of newly appointed Housing Assistants has been assigned to your project. Of the following, the most important thing for you to do when they report for work on their first day is to   23.____

    A. acquaint them with the general features of the duties they are to perform
    B. allow them to ask questions freely about the conditions of work and the possibilities of advancement
    C. ascertain their sympathy with the social philosophy behind low-rent public housing
    D. distribute a schedule of visits to tenants to acquaint the Housing Assistants with the typical situations they will encounter
    E. inform them about time, sickness, absence and vacation regulations

24. Of the following, the best incentive to better work to employ in the supervision of a recently appointed Housing Assistant is, in general, to compare his present progress with   24.____

    A. previous progress made by him at the project
    B. progress of Housing Assistants of average ability at the project
    C. progress of the least competent Housing Assistant at the project
    D. progress of the most efficient Housing Assistant at the project
    E. progress of Housing Assistants in general at all projects

25. Of the following, the most important basis upon which to evaluate the efficiency of a subordinate is his   25.____

    A. accuracy and promptness in execution of assignments
    B. awareness of the social aspects of the assignments given to him
    C. confidence in the handling of difficult assignments
    D. observance of the rules and regulations of the Authority
    E. relationship with fellow employees

KEY (CORRECT ANSWERS)

1. D
2. C
3. A
4. A
5. B

6. B
7. D
8. C
9. D
10. D

11. C
12. C
13. A
14. C
15. C

16. D
17. C
18. C
19. B
20. B or C

21. B
22. C
23. A
24. A
25. A

TEST 3

DIRECTIONS: Each question or incomplete statement is followed by several suggested answers or completions. Select the one that BEST answers the question or completes the statement. *PRINT THE LETTER OF THE CORRECT ANSWER IN THE SPACE AT THE RIGHT.*

1. A Housing Assistant under your supervision attempts to conceal the fact that he has made an error. Of the following, the most reasonable interpretation of this action is that the

    A. action of the Housing Assistant indicates an independent attitude
    B. desire for concealment of the error demonstrates an antisocial attitude
    C. error was probably a minor one which the Housing Assistant felt did not have to be reported to superior authority
    D. evasion indicates the possibility of an inadequate relationship between you and the Housing Assistant
    E. Housing Assistant does not know the proper procedure to follow

2. A Housing Assistant under your supervision complains that he deserves a higher service rating than the one he received recently. Your review of his work indicates that his work performance was average and that the standard rating he received was a just rating. Of the following, the most appropriate reply to his complaint is to

    A. advise him that he may appeal to the Civil Service Commission for a higher rating
    B. point out the below-average aspects of his work which were not included in his service rating report
    C. tell him not to be too concerned about his rating since he was considered a satisfactory employee
    D. tell him that the Departmental Personnel Board, and not you, is responsible for the allocation of service ratings
    E. tell him why his work was considered average and did not deserve more than a standard rating

3. A subject which is LEAST desirable as a topic in group discussion of interviewing problems is

    A. effect of the setting of an interview on the success of the interview
    B. evaluation of the interviews handled by the least efficient staff member
    C. handling language difficulties at interviews
    D. maximum utilization of application forms on which interviews are based
    E. subjective attitudes of applicants for low-rent public housing

4. A Housing Assistant criticizes a form which has been used in connection with applications for low-rent housing as poor because it limits the interviewer to specified areas of discussion with applicants. Of the following, the most appropriate course of action for you, as his supervisor, to take is to

    A. ascertain the need for further guidance of this Housing Assistant by reviewing his past use of this form
    B. ask the Housing Assistant to explain the limitations of the form in relation to required job performance

C. make a study of records of interviews by other Housing Assistants to determine the validity of the criticism
D. tell the Housing Assistant that such limitation is necessary to avoid interviews of undue length
E. tell the Housing Assistant that the ability of an employee to adhere to the form in his interviews is related to his understanding of standard procedures

5. One of your Housing Assistants has shown himself to be inaccurate in checking tenant income records. The action most likely to result in improvement in the work habits of this employee is to

   A. assign him to work that will not require close attention to details
   B. have him study a group of tenant income records which have been accurately checked
   C. review with him some of the records he has checked
   D. tell him that it is just as easy to do his job the right way
   E. warn that he will receive an unsatisfactory rating if he persists in being careless

6. Assume that a new procedure of interviewing has been adopted by the management division which you think may meet with some staff resistance. To reduce such possible resistance to a minimum, the best of the following steps to take is to

   A. advise the staff that they will have to accept the new procedure regardless of their personal feelings about it
   B. appoint a staff committee to study the procedure and report on its objectionable and desirable features
   C. ask staff members who in the past have been resistant to new procedures to comment on the new procedure before it is effective
   D. hold a staff meeting to discuss the meaning and application of the procedure prior to the date it is effective
   E. issue detailed instructions on the use of the new procedure to facilitate its application

7. To determine if assignments made to employees under your supervision are being carried out, the most practical supervisory method is to

   A. develop work-flow charts for use in checking work performance
   B. establish production quotas and work schedules
   C. evaluate periodic reports of work performed by subordinates
   D. give detailed instructions for all work assignments and delegate authority for work performance
   E. keep subordinates under constant surveillance to see that details of assignments are executed properly

8. "Samples of income re-examination records of Housing Assistants, in which no change in income or eligibility is involved, should be reviewed periodically." Of the following, the LEAST important reason for such periodic review is to

   A. correct errors in the application of re-examination procedures
   B. indicate a basis for efficiency ratings of these employees
   C. insure uniformity in application of re-examination procedures

D. obtain data as to the need for further training of Housing Assistants in eligibility review procedures
E. provide a means of determining the comparative production of each Housing Assistant

9. Suppose that a study is to be made of the adequacy of work schedules for maintenance personnel at your project. Of the following, the best first step to take is to

    A. arrange for detailed surveys of actual performance to obtain needed data
    B. discuss current work schedules with the building superintendent and his assistant superintendents
    C. have each employee submit a statement of his daily tasks and the time required for each task
    D. review typical work schedules of other projects to provide the basis for desired standards of work output
    E. utilize records of complaints as to service and breakdown of equipment as the starting point of the study

10. Of the following, the most important reason for planning work schedules for subordinates is that

    A. coverage of essential operations is more likely to be maintained
    B. emergency situations can be handled more expeditiously
    C. subordinates are more likely to be satisfied with their assignments if routinized
    D. supervisory relationships will be clarified and strengthened
    E. the basis for most tenant complaints will be eliminated

11. An employee under your supervision has shown difficulty in organizing his work. Consequently, the quality and quantity of his work output has been below acceptable standards. Of the following, the most effective way of improving the performance of this employee is to

    A. advise the employee to set up a tickler system so that he will not forget essential tasks
    B. encourage the employee to organize his work more efficiently
    C. explain the relationship of proper organization of work to work output
    D. help the employee discover the factors that may be hindering effective organization of work
    E. lay out the work of the employee until he is able to organize his work properly by himself

12. Suppose you have been assigned as site manager of a newly acquired slum clearance site. Of the following, the first major task you should undertake is to

    A. approach community agencies to solicit aid in tenant relocation
    B. establish criteria for determination of usability of residential buildings for which demolition may be deferred
    C. establish procedures for the acceptance from site tenants of applications for permanent low-rent housing
    D. establish reasonable time limits for removal of tenants from the site
    E. plan and administer a complete tenant and physical inventory

13. While walking down the steps of one of the project buildings, you notice a porter doing his work very poorly. Of the following, the proper action for you to take is to

    A. advise the building superintendent that the porter did not seem to know how to do his work
    B. analyze the porter's record to determine if it is satisfactory
    C. inform the building superintendent that a training program for porters appears advisable
    D. question the porter to ascertain whether he knows the proper way to do the job
    E. tell the porter that he is delinquent in his duties

14. After an accident has occurred and the injured employee has been given needed care, it is accepted practice to make a thorough determination of the cause of the accident. From the viewpoint of management, the most important purpose of such accident investigations is to

    A. establish the extent of liability of management in each case
    B. indicate to maintenance employees their responsibility in accident prevention
    C. maintain the morale of the staff and tenants
    D. obtain the necessary data for the liability insurer
    E. prevent the recurrence of such accidents

15. When a congested urban slum area is given over to a private or public housing project, the setting aside, at the same time, of additional space for school building is

    A. undesirable because it tends to decrease the amount of tax-producing property and thereby increase the tax burden on other property owners
    B. undesirable because the location of a school building depends on other additional factors which can be better determined at a later date
    C. desirable because property owners in the area raise fewer objections when land is condemned for both project and school at the same time
    D. desirable because suitable land may otherwise not be readily available for this purpose
    E. desirable because a school is an essential part of the community

16. The most important reason why Housing Assistants should be acquainted with the significant social foci of the housing project neighborhood is that

    A. a more constructive approach for the improvement of intra-family relations may be obtained
    B. better relations between project families and neighborhood families may be fostered
    C. fewer referrals to social agencies will need to be made
    D. neighborhood needs may be assessed more adequately
    E. tenants may be better advised how to budget their incomes

17. The most important positive result of tenant organization from the viewpoint of management is that it

    A. acts as a control on the possible slipshod work of subordinate members of the staff
    B. enables management to avoid complaints of an individual nature
    C. inevitably serves as a filter through which only important tenant problems affecting general welfare pass on to management

D. provides a means for bringing problems to the surface which otherwise might not be known or understood by management
E. usually engages the interests of tenants who will assume positions of leadership in the community

18. Where imminence of eviction of an applicant makes it impracticable to schedule a housing investigation, it is essential that prior to acceptance as an emergency applicant in a permanent project, he submit

    A. conclusive proof of residence at the address from which he is being evicted
    B. detailed proof of income eligibility
    C. evidence that he is unable to find suitable quarters pending completion of the housing investigation
    D. primary proof of citizenship
    E. proof that he is financially responsible or is a recipient of public assistance

19. When the building superintendent tells you that the transformer of one of the oil burners is defective, he is referring to the device which

    A. atomizes the liquid oil prior to ignition
    B. changes low-pressure steam to high-pressure steam
    C. increases the voltage for oil ignition
    D. regulates oil temperature prior to atomization
    E. supplies the proper voltage for operation of the motor

20. When a building superintendent reports corroded flashings resulting in leakage, the part of the building he is referring to is the

    A. basement piping
    B. boiler room
    C. pavement adjoining building
    D. roof
    E. stair halls

21. If an automatic elevator is not leveling properly at floor stops, the proper action to take is to

    A. allow the car to remain in service only if the distance between the car floor and floor landing is 3 inches or less
    B. post signs in the elevator to warn passengers
    C. station a maintenance man near the ground floor stop to warn passengers
    D. take the car out of service during slow periods to make necessary adjustments
    E. take the car out of service immediately to make necessary adjustments

22. Although rock salt is commonly used on the walks of the project when they are iced or heavily packed with snow, the chief disadvantage of its use is that it

    A. creates a very slushy condition
    B. generally causes deterioration of concrete walks
    C. increases cleaning costs if used intensively
    D. is harmful to adjacent trees and shrubs
    E. tends to increase the accident hazard

23. When instructing tenants how to clean enamel-painted woodwork, the tenant should be advised to wash the surfaces with

    A. ammonia water
    B. mild soap and water solution
    C. plain warm water
    D. strong soda solution
    E. vinegar and water solution

24. Of the following items included in the work schedule of porters, the one that should be assigned as a daily duty is

    A. cleaning incinerators
    B. cleaning stairhall windows and woodwork
    C. mopping all assigned stairhalls
    D. sweeping all stair landings
    E. washing down all sidewalks adjacent to assigned buildings

25. Some housing projects have, in the past, reduced their personnel cost for community activities by using tenant volunteers. The major disadvantage of this practice is that

    A. volunteers have no financial ties to oblige them to carry on the work regularly and efficiently
    B. tenant volunteers may not be aware of the most desirable methods of group work
    C. tenant volunteers are usually unable to obtain the respect and cooperation of fellow tenants
    D. demands of tenants for further participation in management operation will be fostered
    E. antagonism between tenant volunteers and tenants using community facilities is a general occurrence

26. "Studies in the cities of Hartford, Chicago, Philadelphia, Newark and New York showed that the rate of juvenile delinquency was highest in areas where housing was least adequate."
    On the basis of this quotation, it is most correct to say that

    A. no relationship can be established at all since bad housing is but one factor among many that may cause delinquent behavior
    B. areas of substandard housing are generally areas of high juvenile delinquency
    C. provision of adequate housing is probably the most effective tool in combating juvenile delinquency
    D. slum areas are less effectively policed than other areas in the cities mentioned
    E. the physical aspects of housing have direct causal relationship with the rate of juvenile delinquency

In questions 27 through 30, each paragraph contains five words in **bold** type, one of which is not in keeping with the meaning of the selection. In the space provided, write the letter of the one of the five words given that does not belong as written in the statement.

27. "The **minimum** amount that can be paid by the **Federal** government in any year as annual **contributions** to a low-rent housing project under a given contract of financial aid is a **fixed** percentage of the total **development** cost of the project."

    A. minimum   B. Federal   C. contributions   D. fixed
    E. development

27._____

28. "The existence and **dimensions** of the slums had long been **recognized** by State legislatures and municipalities, but these local public bodies and officers had **wasted** their efforts primarily on **unintegrated** remedial measures **restricted** in character to building and health codes."

    A. dimensions   B. recognized   C. wasted   D. unintegrated
    E. restricted

28._____

29. "One of the **major** purposes of a program of land **assembly** for urban redevelopment is to direct the location of new **home** building to **zoned** city land by erasing the margin that seems to favor unused **fringe** land."

    A. major   B. assembly   C. home   D. zoned
    E. fringe

29._____

30. Migration of **non-farm** families is estimated to **increase** the needs for housing construction only to the extent that **out-migration** from individual localities is so great as to leave an actual **deficit** of standard housing in those localities **after** demolition of all sub-standard units."

    A. non-farm   B. increase   C. out-migration   D. deficit
    E. after

30._____

KEY (CORRECT ANSWERS)

1.	D	16.	B
2.	E	17.	D
3.	B	18.	A
4.	B	19.	C
5.	C	20.	D
6.	D	21.	E
7.	C	22.	D
8.	E	23.	B
9.	B	24.	D
10.	A	25.	A
11.	D	26.	B
12.	E	27.	A
13.	A	28.	C
14.	E	29.	D
15.	D	30.	D

EXAMINATION SECTION
TEST 1

DIRECTIONS: Each question or incomplete statement is followed by several suggested answers or completions. Select the one that BEST answers the question or completes the statement. *PRINT THE LETTER OF THE CORRECT ANSWER IN THE SPACE AT THE RIGHT.*

1. The following three statements relate to master keys:
    I. The use of the apartment master key by project maintenance employees is authorized for emergencies which require widespread entrance to apartments
    II. Housing patrolmen receive apartment master keys but not maintenance master keys
    III. Defective or broken master keys must be sent to the Bay View Lock Shop only by registered mail.
   Which of the following choices lists all the foregoing statements that are generally CORRECT?

    A. I only is generally correct.
    B. II only is generally correct.
    C. III only is generally correct.
    D. I and III only are generally correct.

1.____

2. State legislation requires an owner, including the Authority, to install a bell, buzzer, and voice intercommunication system and to install self-closing and self-locking building entrance doors under certain conditions.
   The following three statements relate to such installations:
    I. The Authority is obligated to install such a system only when tenants occupying a majority of the apartments in a building make written request and agree to pay for the cost
    II. Tenants who do not request the installation need not pay for it
    III. Housing managers must meet with the executive committee of the tenant organization to discuss possible installation of the system.
   Which of the following choices list all the foregoing statements that are generally correct?

    A. I and II only are generally correct.
    B. II and III only are generally correct.
    C. I and III only are generally correct.
    D. I, II, and III are generally correct.

2.____

3. The following three statements relate to underoccupied apartments:
    I. A tenant may not be transferred to a smaller apartment unless he is eligible on the basis of income for the smaller apartment
    II. The Authority will pay moving expenses according to its schedule for a non-welfare tenant transferring to a smaller apartment
    III. When underoccupancy arises from death, no attempt to have the tenant move to a smaller apartment should be made for six months.
   Which of the following choices lists all the foregoing statements that are generally CORRECT?

3.____

A. I only is generally correct.
B. II only is generally correct.
C. I and II only are generally correct.
D. II and III only are generally correct.

4. The following three statements relate to the project operating budget:
    I. The second- and third-year figures of the three-year budget may be more of an estimate than those for the first year
    II. Housing managers may consult with technicians in the technical service division about budget matters
    III. Each housing manager and superintendent shall maintain a file to be known as *operating budget preparation folder.*
   Which of the following choices lists all the foregoing statements that are generally CORRECT?

    A. I and II only are generally correct.
    B. II and III only are generally correct.
    C. I and III only are generally correct.
    D. I, II, and III are generally correct.

5. The following three statements relate to apartment visits by housing assistants in subsidized projects:
    I. If there are indications of a problem situation or negligent use of the apartment, the housing assistant must visit all the rooms
    II. The tenant has the option of refusing both the orientation visit made after move-in and the annual visit
    III. If there is no record of poor housekeeping, and at first glance the apartment appears to be in reasonably good order, the housing assistant should limit his inspection to the range and the refrigerator.
   Which of the following choices lists all the foregoing statements that are generally CORRECT?

    A. I only is generally correct.
    B. I and II only are generally correct.
    C. II only is generally correct.
    D. II and III only are generally correct.

6. The following three statements relate to the use of project space for community purposes:
    I. All groups requesting space must first apply to the housing manager
    II. The housing manager must notify the legal department immediately upon the vacating of community space by the lessee or upon a major change in the use of space.
    III. The housing manager must maintain a ledger card for each community space under lease and collect rent for such space.
   Which of the following choices lists all the foregoing statements that are generally CORRECT?

    A. I, II, and III are generally correct.
    B. I and II only are generally correct.
    C. II and III only are generally correct.
    D. I and III only are generally correct.

7. A newspaper reporter calls to interview you about a fire that occurred the previous evening in a tenant's apartment. All their furnishings and clothing were destroyed either through fire or water damage. The family was forced to spend the night with several neighbors. You have been authorized to grant the interview.
   Which of the following statements would be PROPER for you to make?
   The family

   A. has been a problem to management because of poor apartment maintenance
   B. is being moved to a smaller apartment in the project because they are destitute
   C. is being relocated to another apartment because of complaints from neighbors
   D. is being moved into a vacant apartment, since it will take some days to rehabilitate their apartment

7.____

8. A press photographer requests permission to take pictures from the roof of a high-rise building. The housing manager at the project should

   A. reject the request in order to comply with the regulations
   B. reject the request because the Authority has no third-party insurance
   C. check his credentials and request permission from the public relations office
   D. verify his credentials and allow him to photograph from the roof

8.____

9. Assume that the tenant patrol has been very effective in a high-rise building in reducing crime and vandalism. However, an incident involving an argument between two youths brings a crowd to the lobby. A patrol volunteer in the lobby has supported the Puerto Rican boy involved, whereas the tenants congregated support the Chinese boy involved. The police are called to disperse the crowd. Later you receive complaints that the patrol in the lobby mistreats the Chinese boys. The incident seems to have stirred up unrest throughout the building.
   Of the following, the BEST way to handle this problem would be to

   A. investigate the charges and, if verified, disband the patrol
   B. request assistance from the office of community affairs at central office
   C. call in the parents and the boys involved in the incident and discuss continued occupancy reevalua-tions
   D. advise the complaining tenants that the patrol is dedicated to their security

9.____

10. Assume that tenant patrol volunteers in one of your 16 buildings request permission to store their lobby table and chairs in the electric meter room. Unless they can store their equipment, they will give up the work, since none of them is willing to continue cluttering his apartment with this equipment.
    You should reject this request and attempt to find another remedy because

    A. buildings serviced by other patrols do not have similar storage space
    B. you doubt that proper room security can be permanently provided
    C. there might be a temptation to store items other than tables and chairs
    D. it is unlawful to use electric meter rooms for storage

10.____

11. A recommendation to terminate tenancy may be made because of alcoholism where it results in

    A. related medical conditions of a chronic nature
    B. family estrangement leading to divorce proceedings

11.____

C. interference with the proper operations of the project
D. substantial reduction in total family income

12. A guide to tenants furnished by a project may NOT give information concerning the address of the local

   A. medicaid alert office
   B. city hospital
   C. Department of Health clinic
   D. drugstore

13. From time to time, employees have been accused of improper actions or behavior while working in apartments. Therefore, when there is someone in the apartment, it is important that certain rules of conduct be observed.
The one of the following which is NOT such a rule is for employees to

   A. place the official *door knob notice* on the door on entering an apartment
   B. avoid any discussion with children
   C. leave the apartment if anyone appears to be under the influence of liquor
   D. discuss the reason for leaving the door open while working

14. The CHIEF function of the housing manager in dealing with a tenants' association is to

   A. listen to their requests and to advise them on Authority policies
   B. provide leadership in conducting their affairs
   C. attend meetings solely to report their activities to the chief manager
   D. attend meetings to identify certain undesirable militants

15. Certain tenants may keep animals within certain limitations.
The one of the following which is NOT a specific category of such tenants is

   A. mute   B. blind
   C. elderly   D. severely handicapped

16. The project office is being picketed by a number of tenants protesting a recent Authority-wide rent increase. The one of the following that the housing manager is LEAST likely to notify is the

   A. public information division
   B. office of the chief of the administration division
   C. chief manager
   D. department of social and community services

17. As manager of a site clearance project, you learn that a tenant of record had just vacated, leaving in possession persons who have been in occupancy for more than six months.
Consistent with the policy on sharing families, you should

   A. consider the remaining persons as tenants
   B. institute summary holdover proceedings
   C. request a notarized certificate of necessity from the occupants
   D. refer the matter to the legal department for disposition

18. On a site you manage, a residential tenant on firm rent refuses to pay the approved scheduled rent.
    Of the following actions, the one you should take IMMEDIATELY is to

    A. determine whether a rent reduction is justified
    B. institute summary proceedings for non-payment
    C. notify the tenant of the commencement of the one-month penalty period
    D. refer the matter to the chief of site management

19. Referral of the tenant to the social services division is advisable in all of the following situations EXCEPT that of a(n)

    A. elderly tenant disturbing her neighbors by irrational behavior
    B. young mother separated from her husband complaining that her worker is not responsive to her needs
    C. tenant admitting that she cannot control the disruptive behavior of her ten-year-old twins
    D. young mother separated from her husband being the subject of frequent complaints by several neighbors in reference to unreasonably noisy parties

20. Submission of a tenant's record to the office of the tenancy administrator for termination review is mandatory when a

    A. tenant's son is arrested for selling narcotics off-project
    B. tenant is arrested for assaulting his wife with his fists
    C. tenant's brother is arrested for possession of marijuana in a neighborhood youth center
    D. tenant is arrested for forgery of his sister's signature

21. A housing police patrolman requests supper money because he worked a tour of 8:00 M. to 8:00 P.M. The overtime was a result of his arresting a suspect caught leaving an apartment with the tenant's television set.
    You are obliged to REJECT the request because

    A. the housing police are not granted supper money in any circumstances
    B. the management petty cash funds cannot be used for police work
    C. the officer was off duty at 8:00 P.M., and it was unreasonable to expect supper money
    D. only his sergeant may authorize such supper money

22. The housing police have submitted an incident report to you involving a tenant of a neighboring project. It is a minor incident which took place in your project and which also involved several of your tenants.
    Of the following actions, you are REQUIRED to

    A. request an interview with the non-tenant at his convenience
    B. write a letter to the non-tenant warning of penalties if the incident recurs
    C. notify the other manager and send a copy of the incident report
    D. arrange with the other manager for a joint conference

23. The housing police apprehend a 12-year-old boy, living in the project, chipping away at the elevator buttons in the lobby and defacing the wall tiles. The damage is thereafter repaired at a cost of $75. The responsible tenant refuses to pay for this damage.
In order to recover the expense of this unlawful destruction, the housing manager may

    A. institute a civil damage suit in small claims court
    B. ask the chief manager to evaluate whether a civil damage suit should be brought
    C. include the charge in a dispossession for non-payment of rent
    D. refer the responsible tenant to the social services division for consultation

24. Assume that the housing police advise you that a tenant has been found murdered in his apartment.
The FIRST action you should take is to

    A. call the local police precinct
    B. notify the president of the tenants' association
    C. call the public relations division
    D. notify the legal division

25. Data show a relationship between felony rates in housing projects and certain other factors. This data showed that, in projects with well-structured moderate-income families, the felony rate per 1,000 families

    A. *falls* as the density of dwelling units per acre increases
    B. *rises* as the density of dwelling units per acre decreases
    C. *falls* as the height of buildings increases
    D. *rises* as the height of buildings increases

KEY (CORRECT ANSWERS)

1.	A	11.	C
2.	C	12.	D
3.	B	13.	D
4.	D	14.	A
5.	A	15.	C
6.	D	16.	D
7.	D	17.	A
8.	C	18.	B
9.	B	19.	B
10.	D	20.	A

21.	A
22.	C
23.	B
24.	C
25.	D

TEST 2

DIRECTIONS: Each question or incomplete statement is followed by several suggested answers or completions. Select the one that BEST answers the question or completes the statement. *PRINT THE LETTER OF THE CORRECT ANSWER IN THE SPACE AT THE RIGHT.*

1. Assume that a housing manager of a large subsidized project advised her senior teller to have the petty cash fund available for inspection on the afternoon of the third Wednesday of the month.
   This practice is considered to be

   A. *desirable* because such an inspection will not interfere with the bookkeeping office when rent is being collected
   B. *undesirable* because an audit of the petty cash fund should be unannounced
   C. *desirable* because it will encourage a better relationship between the manager and the teller
   D. *undesirable* because the third Wednesday may be a welfare check day

   1.____

2. The Authority carries insurance policies for indemnification against certain losses or damages.
   The one of the following for which the Authority is NOT insured is

   A. damage caused by a strike
   B. claims by persons other than employees, including damages for care and loss of services
   C. coverage for alteration of any check, draft, or promissory note
   D. protection against claims by tenants for damage to personal property by employees

   2.____

3. Assume that, as housing manager, you are presented with contract papers which require your signature before payment can be made. The papers are for partial payment for roofing work at a total cost of $50,000. The superintendent and the plant services inspector have already signed, indicating that work has been satisfactorily completed to date.
   Of the following, the BEST reason for you to sign the papers is that

   A. the signatures of the superintendent and the inspector assure that payment is in order
   B. the superintendent has requested you to sign the papers immediately to insure prompt payment
   C. you are satisfied that the work to date complies with the contract
   D. the rules of the Authority requires that the manager sign that he is aware of the progress of the work

   3.____

4. You have posted on the bulletin board in the bookkeeping office information issued by the Treasury Department giving descriptions of counterfeit $20 bills in circulation. The branch bank handling the project account advises you that the previous night's deposit contained a counterfeit $20 bill.
   The one of the following actions you should take is to

   A. request the cashier who accepted the bill to make restitution
   B. request the cashier who accepted the bill to process a shortage adjustment report and sign it

   4.____

C. call the U.S. Treasury Department to report the matter
D. call the housing police for assistance in tracing the passer

5. An aged tenant of the project requests that the teller cash a city payroll check for $287.50 made out to his wife. The check bears the wife's endorsement and the tenant endorses the check in front of the teller. He does not wish to pay his rent at this time. The teller cashes the check.
The teller's action is

   A. *correct;* city payroll checks in any amount should be cashed for tenants
   B. *correct;* this tenant was entitled to have this check cashed
   C. *incorrect;* the tenant should have presented his wife's authorization on a consent to second-party payee form
   D. *incorrect;* the check was payable only to the tenant's spouse

6. Assume that, at the project, a stalled elevator is brought down to floor level. None of the passengers has suffered injury, appear to be in shock or request medical attention. They leave the elevator in a normal manner. One of the passengers is carrying a sleeping infant in her arms.
In this situation, you should GENERALLY

   A. refer adult passengers to the legal department
   B. refrain from submitting a report of the incident
   C. submit a report of accident, public liability
   D. telephone the insurance adjuster for specific instructions

7. A charge may PROPERLY be imposed on tenants for

   A. certain instances of repainting
   B. minor repairs when a tenant is vacating
   C. a transfer to an apartment of a different size to conform to occupancy standards
   D. repair of two leaking faucets

8. A project audit by the audit section of the control department reveals a large number of discrepancies between the E.D.P. listings of tools, equipment, and material and the physical inventory.
Of the following, the LEAST desirable action to take in this situation is to

   A. review all procedures relating to issuing tools and withdrawals from the storeroom
   B. call the housing police detective squad to investigate
   C. institute a semi-annual internal audit covering all accountable items
   D. review storage security

9. The one of the following which is CONSISTENT with the policies and procedures for prevention and elimination of pest and rodent infestation is that

   A. all vacated apartments should be treated for roach infestation
   B. the foreman of pest control operators must inspect the personal property of all intra-project transfer tenants for infestation
   C. in cases of serious infestation the tenant may be required to empty all closets
   D. if no infestation is found in a routine inspection, the premises are not treated

10. You have learned that the maintenance men refuse to make a repair in an apartment because of what they consider filthy housekeeping.
    Of the following actions, the one which would be BEST for you to take FIRST is to

    A. write a letter to the tenant explaining the reason the repair has not been made
    B. send a work order to the superintendent, asking that it be returned showing when the work was completed
    C. inform the superintendent of the situation, and advise him of management's responsibility to make the repair
    D. direct the maintenance men to follow up on the housekeeping problem to insure compliance before the work is done

10._____

11. Tenants who wish to install their own refrigerators in place of refrigerators provided by the Authority may do so subject to certain regulation.
    The one of the following statements which is such a regulation is that

    A. requests for installation of tenant-owned refrigerators must be submitted to the superintendent for approval
    B. refrigerators with dual temperature controls are not permitted
    C. only extension cords bearing U.L. approval may be used between refrigerators and wall outlets
    D. tenant-owned refrigerators may be installed only in kitchens

11._____

12. A tenant complains to you that the painter shattered a $50 mirror. The tenant requests payment for the mirror. The painter is an employee of the contractor and not of the Authority.
    The one of the following actions that you should take in handling this complaint is to

    A. approve a property damage claim for 90% of the loss
    B. refer the tenant to the contractor to whom she should present her claim
    C. advise the contractor of the claim and request that the tenant be paid
    D. prepare and submit to the legal department a notice of claim

12._____

13. In the event of fire in the boiler plant, the FIRST step to take is to

    A. fight the fire with the prescribed fire extinguisher
    B. ask the first person passing by to call the Fire Department
    C. activate the nearest Fire Department alarm box
    D. pull the remote control switch

13._____

14. Assume that a boiler explosion has occurred. The resulting damage is less than $700.
    Of the following actions, the one which the manager should take FIRST is to

    A. consult with the chief of insurance
    B. proceed through the superintendent to repair or restore the premises
    C. request a performance bond from a designated outside contractor
    D. report the problem to the state division of housing and community renewal

14._____

15. Top priority in snow removal must be given to

    A. clearing ramps and interior secondary sidewalks
    B. providing access to fuel lines and fire hydrants
    C. building entrance steps and entrance landings
    D. interior sidewalks leading from buildings directly to perimeter sidewalks

15._____

16. A housing manager may approve a request for an inter-project transfer when the tenant

    A. who is the principal wage-earner was transferred two months ago to a new work location requiring two hours' traveling time
    B. who has a chronic illness or a physical handicap requires specialized care or facilities not available near the project
    C. is in an overcrowded apartment because a daughter who was an original member of the family has returned home with her husband
    D. in a middle-income project requests a transfer to a subsidized project because he has been on strike for two months

17. The assistant housing manager requests your advice, as housing manager, about an unauthorized occupancy. A daughter and her two children have moved into a tenant's apartment. The tenant family consists of husband, wife, and teenage son. The tenant is receiving aid from the department of social services and produces evidence that the three additional family members have also been budgeted since their unauthorized move-in about a year ago. Therefore, the tenant should be advised

    A. to seek special permission from the housing consultant for this occupancy arrangement
    B. to tell the three additional occupants to move out and then apply for approval to move into this apartment
    C. that since there has been no change in rent you will approve a change in status
    D. that the Authority considers the family composition to be in violation of occupancy standards

18. Assume that in the course of a regular call to an apartment by an employee a serious quarrel arises among several adults who are in the apartment.
    Of the following, the MOST important rule for the employee to follow is to

    A. observe these persons carefully to determine possible signs of intoxication or of substance abuse
    B. attempt to mediate the dispute so that he may proceed to complete his assigned tasks without interruption
    C. instruct the tenants and their guests, if any, as to their privileges and responsibilities relative to the premises
    D. avoid involvement and, if necessary, leave the apartment

19. For a residual single person to remain in occupancy, he is required to

    A. have reached age 30
    B. be ambulatory
    C. accept immediate transfer to a smaller apartment
    D. pass a monthly apartment inspection for six consecutive months

20. You have evicted a tenant whose entire furnishings have been placed on the street on the order of the marshal, who has given you possession of the apartment.
    Of the following, it would be CORRECT for you to

    A. have the department of sanitation dispose of the street encumbrance
    B. have project personnel dispose of the encumbrance by commercial storage
    C. charge the tenant's account for the cost of removing the encumbrance
    D. charge the tenant on a time basis for removal from the street by project staff

21. Assume that you have decided to recommend termination of tenancy based on non-desirability.
The way in which you should treat the facts or incidents and their sources upon which you relied for your decision should be to

   A. *withhold* the facts, although the source may be revealed to the tenant
   B. *reveal* the facts, although the source need not be revealed to the tenant
   C. *reveal* the facts and the source to the tenant
   D. *withhold* the facts and the source from the tenant

22. A single elderly occupant is found dead in his apartment. You have been unable to locate any relatives or references appearing in the tenant record, despite diligent efforts.
You may, therefore, take possession of the apartment ONLY if

   A. you receive a release from the public administrator's office
   B. there is more than one month's rent in arrears
   C. the furnishings are considered worthless
   D. the police find the keys in the apartment and turn them over to you

23. When a manager decides that a tenant's shades are in such condition that replacement is required, and he provides the tenant with used shades, there shall be _____ charge.

   A. a charge of 3/4 of the scheduled
   B. a charge of 1/2 of the scheduled
   C. a charge of 1/4 of the scheduled
   D. no

24. Certain public agencies are entitled to full disclosure of confidential information concerning tenants or applicants.
One such agency is the State

   A. Crime Victims Compensation Board
   B. Department of Audit and Control
   C. Division of Housing and Community Renewal
   D. Division of Municipal Affairs

25. Assume that you are asked by a local community organization to serve on a special committee which is to select an executive director for the organization. You accept the invitation and subsequently interview several candidates.
Which of the following is the LEAST important consideration in reaching a valid decision about the suitability of each candidate for the position?

   A. Amount and sequence of experience in the candidate's work history
   B. Candidate's behavior during the interview
   C. Inferences concerning the candidate's underlying motives for seeking the position
   D. General qualifications needed for satisfactory job performance by a candidate

KEY (CORRECT ANSWERS)

1.	B	11.	D
2.	A	12.	B
3.	C	13.	D
4.	B	14.	B
5.	B	15.	B
6.	B	16.	B
7.	A	17.	D
8.	B	18.	D
9.	C	19.	B
10.	C	20.	C

21. B
22. A
23. D
24. C
25. C

TEST 3

DIRECTIONS: Each question or incomplete statement is followed by several suggested answers or completions. Select the one that BEST answers the question or completes the statement. *PRINT THE LETTER OF THE CORRECT ANSWER IN THE SPACE AT THE RIGHT.*

1. Authority officials have stressed that crime reported in public housing is proportionately much less than crime reported in the city as a whole. Some critics, however, hold such a comparison to mean little.
   Which of the following statements BEST supports the view of these critics?

   A. In compiling its data, the Authority uses a method different from the uniform crime reporting system of the city's Police Department.
   B. Many crime victims do not report crimes because they fear retaliation by criminals or believe that the police can do nothing.
   C. Recent sharp drops in reported crime have resulted from a temporary increase in security measures in the project.
   D. There are generally more commercial establishments and other inviting targets for criminals outside, rather than inside, housing projects.

1.____

2. The Authority police consider a major impediment to the performance of their duties to be an unacceptably large number of defects in

   A. locks   B. radios
   C. handcuffs   D. ammunition

2.____

3. MOST disagreements between the Authority police and the city police are caused by

   A. differences in salaries
   B. jurisdictional disputes
   C. conflicts concerning peace officer and police officer status
   D. unequal advancement opportunities

3.____

4. Designated employee union representatives are permitted to be released with pay by the housing manager for several purposes.
   For which of the following activities would released time be WITHOUT pay?

   A. Investigation of grievances
   B. Participating in meetings of departmental joint labor relations committees
   C. Negotiating with and appearing before departmental and other city officials and agencies
   D. Attendance at union meetings or conventions

4.____

5. Assume that you are the trial officer in a local disciplinary trial of a maintenance man based on charges by the superintendent that he demanded $2.00 from each tenant for whom he had installed a door-lock chain provided by the tenant. At the hearing, it develops that much more serious wrongdoing appears to have occurred.
   As trial officer, you believe that maximum penalties available to you are inadequate in this case. Of the following action, it would be MOST appropriate for you to

   A. advise the maintenance man to seek competent counsel
   B. impose a separate maximum penalty for each instance of wrongdoing

5.____

C. postpone the trial and present the information to the District Attorney
D. suspend the trial and consult with the Authority's general counsel

6. Monthly toll telephone charges reveal a number of costly personal calls in the sum of $50 traced to an employee. Despite the evidence, the employee denies the accusation and refuses to pay the charges. You decide to hold a local disciplinary hearing.
The one of the following actions you are REQUIRED to take is to

   A. discuss the problem with the chief manager before taking any other action
   B. advise the employee you will be the hearing officer
   C. give the employée a notice of disciplinary charges indicating the charges and time and place of hearing
   D. advise the employee that the technical rules of evidence will be adhered to at the hearing

7. The housing manager has authority to write off claims in favor of or against the Authority within specified amounts. In accordance with this policy, the housing manager may

   A. dispose of any claim by a tenant or former tenant provided the amount of the payment does not exceed $50
   B. dispose of any claim by a tenant or former tenant provided the amount of the payment does not exceed $25
   C. write off any claim against a tenant in residence if the amount does not exceed $25
   D. write off any claim against a former tenant if the amount does not exceed $75

8. The one of the following statements which is CORRECT in reference to assets and eligibility for continued occupancy is that

   A. any tenant whose assets exceed three times the continued occupancy limit for his size apartment is ineligible
   B. a tenant who owns a building which contains a suitable dwelling unit in which he can live is ineligible if his equity in the building exceeds three times the occupancy limit
   C. a tenant whose earning capacity is limited or nonexistent is exempted from any limitation on excess assets for eligibility for continued occupancy provided that the district chief manager approves such exemption
   D. assets are defined to include cash on hand and in banks and the initial purchase value of real property, stocks, and bonds, and other forms of capital investment

9. Families determined as falling within certain categories may be declared ineligible for admission to public housing projects in the absence of extenuating circumstances. The one of the following which is SUCH a category is a family in which a(n)

   A. member of the family was involved in the sale of narcotics more than five years before the rental interview
   B. member of the family is a confirmed addict and is not undergoing follow-up treatment by a professional agency after discharge from an institution
   C. member of the family under the age of sixteen was involved as an offender in a crime of a sexual nature such as rape, carnal abuse, or impairing the morals of a minor
   D. adult member of the family was involved in an act of violence not of a serious criminal nature

10. The TOTAL proportion of apartments painted which the housing manager and the super- 10.____
    intendent should inspect, or have inspected, is usually about

    A. 10% B. 20% C. 30% D. 40%

11. Because of the great demand for housing in the city, some developments have been con- 11.____
    structed on landfill on reclaimed river edges.
    One such project is

    A. Roosevelt Island
    B. Brooklyn Bridge Southwest
    C. Battery Park City
    D. Twin Parks

12. The issue raised by the plaintiffs in the recent legal suit against the Authority regarding 12.____
    the public housing in the Seward Park Extension Urban Renewal Area was the granting
    of preference in tenant selection to

    A. large families
    B. families from outside the area
    C. families of war veterans
    D. non-welfare families

13. *Exclusionary zoning* leads to residential segregation by social class or race. 13.____
    The one of the following MOST likely to lead to exclusionary zoning is for a state to
    permit

    A. apartment units to be of various sizes
    B. low-income housing to be built on private land
    C. municipalities to control building permits
    D. unrelated persons to live together

14. The portion of the Administrative Code that sets minimum standards for decent, safe, 14.____
    and sanitary dwellings is known as the _____ Code.

    A. General Construction   B. Multiple Dwelling
    C. Housing Maintenance   D. Building Standards

15. Of the following, which is the MOST accurate general description of the book, DEFENSI- 15.____
    BLE SPACE, by Oscar Newman?
    The book

    A. is a detailed study of the architectural design of public housing projects in the city
       for the purpose of achieving greater economy of materials
    B. advocates using architectural design to create an environment for the enhance-
       ment of inhabitants' lives while also providing security for their families, neighbors,
       and friends
    C. concludes that a large police force is the major protection against most ordinary
       kinds of crime in public housing
    D. proposes high-rise developments as the rational remedy for chronic housing short-
       ages and the most effective use of urban space

16. In recent years, a number of cities have emphasized the construction of low-rise vest-pocket public housing projects.
    The one of the following which is the MAJOR disadvantage of this type of public housing, compared to larger-scale public housing projects, is that it

    A. has relatively higher tenant-borne operating and maintenance costs
    B. is more likely to encourage criminal activity
    C. inhibits community activities among tenants
    D. must be located at considerable distance from the central city

17. The one of the following which is usually LEAST significant in predicting whether a particular building located in a disadvantaged area of the city will be abandoned is

    A. its condition in comparison to low-income housing in other parts of the city
    B. the cost of maintaining it in good repair
    C. the extent of the drug addiction problem and criminal activity in the immediate neighborhood
    D. the attitude and behavior of the tenants of the particular building

18. The one of the following which is the MOST important cause of the low vacancy rate in public housing in the city in comparison to vacancy rates in other cities is the

    A. similarity in architectural design between public housing and middle-income housing in the city
    B. stringent enforcement in the city of relevant housing codes
    C. greater proximity of public housing in the city to unskilled job markets
    D. relatively large number of households in the city public housing which consist of the working poor

19. Housing experts who advocate the construction of public housing, rental supplements, and similar direct subsidies usually attribute the shortage of adequate housing for low-income families PRIMARILY to

    A. racial discrimination which has resulted in a destructive attitude toward housing on the part of minority group members
    B. the absence of mass production techniques in the building industry
    C. the recurrent lack of mortgage credit
    D. the ability of major cities to mount effective housing programs

20. A federally-funded program of free legal service, serving persons with poverty-level income, represents many residents of public housing.
    In the city, the program is known as

    A. the Bar Association of the City
    B. the Council Against Poverty
    C. Community Action for Legal Services
    D. the Community Service Society

21. The federal government has recently proposed reducing the rent of newly constructed subsidized units for low-income households and, instead, assisting such households through cash housing allowances.
    This proposed program lacks a provision to

A. give low-income persons freedom to choose where and how to live
B. pay the difference between what low-income persons can afford and the fair rent value of the quarters
C. prohibit landlords from raising rents unduly
D. provide special grants for cities with low vacancy rates

22. The Federal housing policies of the 1960s were LEAST successful in

    A. generating increased housing production
    B. improving conditions in deteriorating neighborhoods
    C. promoting economic stabilization of the housing industry
    D. encouraging home ownership for moderate-income households

22._____

23. The following sentences, when put in correct order, constitute a complete paragraph. Select from among the choices listed below, the one in which the CORRECT order is shown.
    I. Project residents had first claim to this use, followed by surrounding neighborhood children.
    II. By contrast, recreation space within the project's interior was found to be used more often by both groups.
    III. Studies of the use of project grounds in many cities showed grounds left open for public use were neglected and unused, both by residents and by members of the surrounding community.
    IV. Project residents had clearly laid claim to the play spaces, setting up and enforcing unwritten rules for use.
    V. Each group, by experience, found their activities easily disrupted by other groups, and their claim to the use of space for recreation difficult to enforce.
    The CORRECT answer is:

    A. IV, V, I, II, III
    B. V, II, IV, III, I
    C. I, IV, III, II, V
    D. III, V, II, IV, I

23._____

24. The following sentences, when put in correct order, constitute a complete paragraph. Select from among the choices listed below the one in which the CORRECT order is shown.
    I. They do not consider the problems correctable within the existing subsidy formula and social policy of accepting all eligible applicants regardless of social behavior and life style.
    II. A recent survey, however, indicated that tenants believe these problems correctable by local housing authorities and management within the existing financial formula.
    III. Many of the problems and complaints concerning public housing management and design have created resentment between the tenant and the landlord.
    IV. This same survey indicated that administrators and managers do not agree with the tenants.
    The CORRECT answer is:

    A. II, I, III, IV
    B. I, III, IV, II
    C. III, II, IV, I
    D. IV, II, I, III

24._____

25. The following sentences, when put in correct order, constitute a complete paragraph. Select from among the choices listed below the one in which the CORRECT order is shown.

   I. In single family residences, there is usually enough distance between tenants to prevent occupants from annoying one another.
   II. For example, a certain small percentage of tenant families has one or more members addicted to alcohol.
   III. While managers believe in the right of individuals to live as they choose, the manager becomes concerned when the pattern of living jeopardizes others' rights.
   IV. Still others turn night into day, staging lusty entertainments which carry on into the hours when most tenants are trying to sleep.
   V. In apartment buildings, however, tenants live so closely together that any misbehavior can result in unpleasant living conditions.
   VI. Other families engage in violent argument.

The CORRECT answer is:

A. III, II, V, IV, VI, I
B. I, V, II, VI, IV, III
C. II, V, IV, I, III, VI
D. IV, II, V, VI, III, I

KEY (CORRECT ANSWERS)

1. D
2. B
3. B
4. D
5. D

6. C
7. B
8. C
9. B
10. B

11. C
12. B
13. C
14. C
15. B

16. A
17. A
18. D
19. C
20. C

21. C
22. B
23. D
24. C
25. B

EXAMINATION SECTION
TEST 1

DIRECTIONS: Each question or incomplete statement is followed by several suggested answers or completions. Select the one that BEST answers the question or completes the statement. *PRINT THE LETTER OF THE CORRECT ANSWER IN THE SPACE AT THE RIGHT.*

1. The reason that increases in maintenance charges are as large, on the average, for cooperative tenant-owners as increases in rents for rental tenants is that

   A. most cooperative buildings maintain a higher level of service than similar rental buildings
   B. the cooperative buildings are older and need more repair and maintenance
   C. the tenant-owners have tended to seek higher profits from their investments
   D. unions representing staff of cooperative buildings have won larger contract settlements

2. Although *domicile* and *residence* are used interchangeably, the legal distinction between these terms is that *domicile* is a

   A. fixed place of habitation, while *residence* is a transient place of dwelling
   B. term considered obsolete, while *residence* is proper legal usage
   C. precise legal term, while *residence* is a popular term with a similar meaning
   D. transient place of dwelling, while *residence* is fixed place of habitation

3. The legal minimum wage of janitors is fixed by the

   A. Office of Collective Bargaining   B. State Labor Law
   C. Multiple Dwelling Law   D. Amended Rent Law

4. Housing which is built by private industry and then purchased by the city for low-income use is known as _____ housing.

   A. contingent   B. custodial   C. operational   D. turnkey

5. A building which is *gutted* so that only the walls and beams remain is usually referred to, in the rent and eviction regulations, as _____ demolished.

   A. completely   B. substantially   C. reasonably   D. virtually

6. *Tinning* is a term generally used to describe the

   A. aluminum curtain walls of modern office buildings
   B. installation of wire lathing
   C. covering of windows in buildings with sheet metal
   D. use of substandard materials in building repairs

7. The CHIEF purpose of an electric fuse is to

   A. assure better service by diminishing power failures
   B. connect the house wiring to the main power lines
   C. break the circuit when the electric wiring system is overloaded
   D. provide for a more even distribution of electric power throughout the wiring system

8. With respect to residential tenants, when the outside temperature between six a.m. and ten p.m., is below 55 degrees, heat must be kept AT LEAST at _____ degrees.

   A. 66 B. 68 C. 70 D. 72

9. With respect to residential tenants, when the outside temperature between ten p.m. and six a.m., is below 40 degrees, heat must be kept AT LEAST at _____ degrees.

   A. 55 B. 57 C. 59 D. 61

10. The city rent stabilization law provides that increases in rent for rent stabilized apartments are to be determined by the

    A. housing and development administrator
    B. board of standards and appeals
    C. commissioner of rent and housing maintenance
    D. rent guidelines board

11. The price index used to determine proper increases in rent under the rent stabilization law has as its MAIN components

    A. fuel costs and labor costs
    B. fuel costs and real property taxes
    C. labor costs and real property taxes
    D. personal income taxes and municipal taxes

12. With reference to dwelling units covered, the rent stabilization law requires the landlord to

    A. take additional security measures
    B. use the same form of fuel as previously
    C. continue all previous services
    D. refrain from discharging any employee

13. Fines imposed on landlords for violating housing codes have failed to result in improved housing conditions PRIMARILY because the fines are

    A. passed on to the tenants in the form of higher rents
    B. such a heavy financial burden that the landlords cannot afford to improve their property
    C. set aside by appeal to the courts
    D. so small as to constitute a license rather than a deterrent

14. An *arm's length* transaction is one that is

    A. autonomous   B. fixed
    C. cautious   D. hazardous

15. The means by which a legal or equitable title to real estate is transferred is known as

    A. conversion   B. conveyance
    C. devolution   D. replevin

16. When the city offers property for sale which is no longer needed for a public improvement, an *upset price* is listed in the offering.
    This figure is the

    A. amount that the city expects to receive in tax arrears
    B. price at which bids may be expected
    C. minimum price acceptable under the terms of the offering
    D. assessed valuation of the property

17. The process of leveling or adjusting the assessments of individual taxpayers, so that the property of one shall not be assessed at a higher or lower percentage of its market value than the property of another, is known as

    A. equalized responsibility assessment
    B. equalized assessed valuation
    C. equitable exclusion assessment
    D. equitable recoupment valuation

18. As applied to housing, of the following, the term *restrictive convenant* means, MOST NEARLY

    A. a planned and orderly proportional admission of blacks to previously segregated residential areas
    B. a state or local law requiring racial residential segregation
    C. an agreement by property owners in a neighborhood not to sell or rent their property to members of specific minority groups
    D. the organized use of such devices as persuasion and violence to segregate the residents in a community

19. A federally-funded program in the city that requires widespread citizen participation in the program and maximum opportunities for employing residents in the area in all phases of the program is carried out by the

    A. Department of City Planning
    B. Department of Consumer Affairs
    C. Model Cities Administration
    D. Environmental Protection Administration

20. A State agency, having broad powers which enable it to condemn land and to build structures that may violate local zoning and building regulations, together with broad borrowing capacity from state bonds, is the

    A. Job Development Authority
    B. Urban Development Corporation
    C. Office of Planning Coordination
    D. Dormitory Authority

21. Nearly two-thirds of all non-white families in the central cities today live in substandard housing amid urban blight.
    This is so MAINLY because most non-white families are

    A. serious problems to social service agencies
    B. headed by a male
    C. conditioned to self-segregation
    D. unable to pay the rent necessary for adequate housing

22. The multiple dwelling law requires that where an owner does not reside in the premises, a janitor or person responsible to the owner must reside in or within 200 feet of a multiple dwelling whenever the number of families occupying the building is _____ or more families.

    A. 6   B. 13   C. 20   D. 24

23. Of the following, the FUNDAMENTAL standard for measuring effectiveness in urban renewal should be expressed in terms of

    A. economy and efficiency
    B. the degree of community control
    C. the maximum utilization of vacant land
    D. meeting social needs

24. Most of the older apartment units in the city contain lead-based paint.
    Of the following, the statement which is NOT true about such paint is:

    A. Children one to six years of age are the primary victims of lead poisoning and more than 80% of cases occur in children between 18 and 36 months
    B. The recommended method of preventing poisoning is by painting over the lead-based paint with modern, non-toxic paint.
    C. Lead poisoning resulting from ingestion of lead-based paint most often occurs in poor neighborhoods.
    D. The lead-poisoning problem is now known to many more persons and this knowledge has promoted remedial action.

25. In the past few years there has been a rapid increase in the number of rental buildings converted to cooperative ownership.
    Of the following, the MOST compelling reason for this trend is that

    A. an owner can thereby generally get two or three times as much for a building from conversion than from selling it
    B. such ownership is a valuable approach to the preservation of good housing and encourages the middle-class to remain
    C. tenants have become increasingly eager to gain control of their apartments to prevent abandonment or deterioration
    D. the sponsor is required to guarantee refund of the purchase price if the tenant exercises his option to withdraw within one year

26. Recently enacted legislation affecting air pollution prohibits in new residential construction the use of

    A. dumbwaiters   B. incinerators
    C. compactors   D. private janitorial collection

27. The modular-type of prefabricated housing has recently gained support as a partial remedy to the housing shortage. However, the use of such housing has encountered obstacles.
Of the following, the statement which does NOT describe an obstacle is:

   A. Safety experts have voiced grave concern about the dangers of collapse or fire relative to such structures.
   B. Building codes in many cities have hampered the use of such standard units.
   C. Labor unions have sometimes been reluctant to accept such housing because it reduces work time and the work force.
   D. Demand for such housing has been too light to make mass production economically feasible.

28. In the city, rooming houses which are converted to multiple dwellings are subject to real estate tax abatement PRIMARILY because

   A. it is considered socially desirable to encourage the upgrading of decaying properties
   B. landlords of multiple dwellings are less likely to abandon such properties
   C. the number of elderly persons seeking apartments in preference to rooming houses has increased
   D. the multiple dwellings will provide housing for a greater number of persons

29. The *New York Plan* for speeding the entry of minority group members into the building construction trades has been criticized severely in the press and by a major civil rights organization because

   A. any attempt to increase the rate of minority group employment is difficult in a period of rising joblessness
   B. it fails to provide assurances that any of the trainees will get either union membership or regular work
   C. it requires the employment of only one trainee for every four journeymen employed
   D. its stringent penalties needlessly antagonize the unions which are honestly seeking to overcome racial bias

30. Department rules and regulations should try to anticipate all the situations that might arise involving courteous behavior, and should attempt to provide specific rules to cover all such circumstances.
This statement, is GENERALLY

   A. *false,* there is no practical limit to the possible situations which involve courteous behavior
   B. *false;* the provision of specific rules will encourage minimum standards of courteous behavior and discourage the development of higher standards
   C. *true;* such specific rules and regulations will eliminate excuses for discourteous behavior
   D. *true;* the courteous behavior of employees is the most important aspect of a public relations program

31. For a supervisor to inform his staff about the reasons for a particular policy of the agency is

   A. *unwise;* mainly because the rent inspectors may disagree with the policy
   B. *unwise;* mainly because the rent inspectors may apply the policy too leniently
   C. *wise;* mainly because the rent inspectors are more likely to apply the policy correctly
   D. *wise;* mainly because the rent inspectors will feel that they set agency policy

32. The most important, SINGLE criterion of a sound performance evaluation program for rent inspectors is whether it

   A. fosters the development of good employee performance
   B. provides a comprehensive record of behavior as possible evidence in disciplinary proceedings
   C. increases the awareness of subordinates that departmental rules must be followed
   D. properly delegates authority through the committee method of rating

33. A supervisor has a practice of distributing agendas to all rent inspectors the day before a staff meeting is to be held.
   In general, this practice is

   A. *good;* meetings will be more orderly because less controversy will follow
   B. *good;* rent inspectors can give prior thought to the matters to be discussed
   C. *bad;* the problem of maintaining order is made more difficult because every rent inspector will want to talk
   D. *bad;* rent inspectors will be less spontaneous and candid in their discussions

34. While conducting group discussions with rent inspectors, the supervisor should observe all of the following practice EXCEPT that of

   A. making the rent inspectors aware that he accepts them personally, even when he questions specific statements
   B. establishing and developing mutual confidence between himself and the rent inspectors
   C. keeping the rent inspectors directed toward the goal of the meeting
   D. allowing the least knowledgeable rent inspectors to direct the group

35. Periodic training of rent inspectors, experienced as well as entrants, is a necessary requirement for effective operations
   This statement is GENERALLY

   A. *true;* the original training may be forgotten or made obsolete by changing conditions and improved methods
   B. *true;* experienced rent inspectors and entrants all require continued training at essentially the same level
   C. *false;* such training would undermine the morale of the experienced rent inspectors and seriously affect their performance
   D. *false;* methods of operation are usually stable and therefore additional training is unnecessary

KEY (CORRECT ANSWERS)

1.	A	16.	C
2.	A	17.	B
3.	B	18.	C
4.	D	19.	C
5.	B	20.	B
6.	C	21.	D
7.	C	22.	B
8.	B	23.	D
9.	A	24.	B
10.	D	25.	A
11.	C	26.	B
12.	C	27.	A
13.	D	28.	A
14.	A	29.	B
15.	B	30.	A

31. C
32. A
33. B
34. D
35. A

TEST 2

DIRECTIONS: Each question or incomplete statement is followed by several suggested answers or completions. Select the one that *BEST* answers the question or completes the statement. *PRINT THE LETTER OF THE CORRECT ANSWER IN THE SPACE AT THE RIGHT.*

1. A tenant who is unlawfully removed by a landlord from any housing accommodation may within two years from the date of occurrence bring a civil action against the landlord by reason of such unlawful removal.
   In such cases the landlord's maximum liability may be reasonable attorney's fees and costs as determined by the court and

   A. the full loss suffered by the tenant
   B. the cost of removal assumed by the tenant
   C. twice the stipends paid for relocation of the tenant
   D. three times the damages sustained

   1.____

2. An order requiring a landlord to paint an apartment shall set forth the interval for the apartment to be repainted. Of the following, the MAJOR reason for this requirement is that

   A. the tenant could otherwise make an application for a decrease in rent based upon substantial deterioration of service
   B. landlords may pyramid delays by not painting at fixed intervals
   C. the housing accommodations could suffer a reduction in rental value if this requirement were not imposed
   D. maximum rents would be affected by the alteration of the painting schedule

   2.____

3. A landlord claims that, without his knowledge or consent, a stranger was able to occupy a recently vacated apartment. The landlord wishes to evict this stranger.
   Of the following, the *ONLY* correct statement is that the landlord

   A. must obtain a certificate of eviction from the city rent agency
   B. can go to court to have the stranger removed
   C. cannot evict the tenant unless he rented the apartment prior to the occupancy of the apartment by the stranger
   D. must not evict the tenant without getting him another apartment

   3.____

4. The city rent agency may order a decrease in rent where there exists a failure to maintain

   A. a normal increase in the rent of uncontrolled accommodations
   B. equipment in accordance with applicable rules and regulations of the National Board of Fire Underwriters
   C. cyclical inspection if equipment
   D. the same dwelling space or essential services as were in existence on the date of determination of the maximum rent

   4.____

5. The administrator may modify or revoke any order issued by him under the regulations or any order issued under previous regulations where he finds that

   5.____

A. such order was the result of illegality, irregularity in vital matters, or fraud
B. the maximum rent in the order is to be subject to a proceeding for judicial review
C. the tenant failed to pay the maximum rent established in the order
D. such order was not received by the tenant in occupancy of the apartment

6. Of the following, the one which is NOT considered a decrease in essential service is 6._____

   A. the absence of an apartment entrance door viewer
   B. a broken glass shower enclosure
   C. an exposed live electrical wire
   D. a broken refrigerator during the summer months

7. Of the following, the ONE condition which may make the landlord ineligible for a rent increase is the fact that 7._____

   A. violations of the building code have been recorded against the property
   B. a portion of the property is leased for commercial use
   C. the landlord received a 15% increase 36 months ago
   D. the property consists solely of single-room occupancy accommodations

8. A rent control form does NOT exist for the purpose of 8._____

   A. registering a housing accommodation
   B. decontrol of a housing accommodation
   C. landlord recovering tenant rent exemption loss
   D. tenant response to a request for a *hardship increase*

9. A tenant is NOT violating a substantial obligation of his tenancy if he 9._____

   A. pays his rent ten or more days late every month
   B. leaves his home unoccupied for a year or more
   C. inflicts willful and serious injury on the landlord
   D. inflicts substantial damage to public halls and lobbies

10. A tenant may refuse access to a landlord if the landlord seeks to 10._____

    A. repair a leaking sink on Sunday
    B. install storm windows during the winter
    C. show the apartment to a prospective tenant
    D. paint the apartment during a snowstorm

11. The director may NOT reduce rents for a landlord's refusal to 11._____

    A. repair a broken stairway
    B. correct a breakdown of equipment
    C. replace a broken window that may have been broken by the tenant
    D. provide a tenant with a new refrigerator

12. A tenant would like her white apartment repainted in white at the required painting time. 12._____
    The landlord wants to use green for uniformity with other apartments.
    The apartment MUST be painted in

    A. white B. green
    C. a neutral or pastel color D. a color acceptable to a third party

13. A landlord refuses to re-wallpaper an apartment at the time he is required to repaint, but offers to paint the rooms instead.
    The landlord has

    A. to do anything the tenant requests in redecorating
    B. the option to repaper or repaint
    C. to do exactly what was done at the last required painting
    D. no choice or he will face a rent reduction

14. A landlord has painted an apartment every three years and the kitchen and bathroom yearly. He decides to discontinue the annual painting of the kitchen and bathroom.
    He is required to paint

    A. every year or face a rent readjustment
    B. as per prior practice or face a rent readjustment
    C. the entire apartment every three years, since his new policy is proper
    D. the entire apartment every two years

15. A tenant removes the poorly functioning one-ton air conditioner from his apartment and replaces it with his
    own of the same size. The landlord seeks a further increase in maximum rent for such replacement by the tenant. The increase will be

    A. *denied,* since the new air conditioner did not increase service
    B. *denied,* since there has been a reduction in the amount of current required
    C. *approved,* because the air conditioner is a new service
    D. *approved,* because the new air conditioner uses more current

16. A new tenant demands painting of rent controlled premises. The landlord painted a year and half before the former tenant vacated.
    Under the rent regulations, the new tenant is entitled to a

    A. rent reduction because the apartment is not in proper condition
    B. rent reduction until his premises are painted
    C. painting if the walls and ceilings are dirty
    D. painting a year and a half after he has moved in

17. A landlord seeks a restoration of rents by correcting a violation. The tenant refuses to allow an examination of his rented premises for the purpose of clearing this violation.
    The result will be that

    A. the tenant can be forced to allow such examination
    B. the landlord can obtain a *certificate of no violations*
    C. the violation will be presumed to have been removed
    D. rents may not be restored until the examination proves that the violation has been corrected

18. A defective stove is reported by a tenant as a possibly dangerous condition.
    The tenant's request for action can be expedited by

    A. a rent examiner only
    B. a supervising rent examiner only
    C. either a rent examiner or a supervising rent examiner
    D. neither of the above

19. A tenant installs a burglar alarm on his door, resulting in a large hole in the door. The landlord demands, in writing, restoration of the door or its original condition. The tenant refuses.
    Of the following, it is CORRECT to say that

    A. this is grounds for a certificate of eviction
    B. this may be a breach of substantial obligation to be resolved by the court
    C. the tenant should not be ordered to restore the door
    D. the landlord may raise the rent by $2.00 per month

20. In cooperation with other city departments to compel a landlord to furnish heat and hot water to housing accommodations in his building, the director may

    A. serve additional notices of violation until the landlord complies
    B. order reduction of the maximum rent by not more than 50%
    C. commence proceedings to reduce the maximum rent to as low as $1.00 per month
    D. advise the tenants not to pay the next month's rent when it becomes due

21. Where tenants' multiple applications for rent reduction are filed and the city rent agency orders a reduction in rent, pursuant to the rent and eviction regulations, due to a reduction in service, this action

    A. does not terminate the tenants' interest in the matter, since other city agencies should be allowed to exercise their appropriate powers
    B. terminates the tenants' interest in the matter, since the restoration of service is not of prime concern
    C. does not terminate the tenants' interest in the matter, since the rent reduction provides a profit motive for a restoration of service
    D. terminates the tenants' interest in the matter, since the tenants have been compensated for reduction of service

22. The schedule of rental values for the modernization or upgrading of an incinerator assumes the granting of tax abatement to the owner for the reasonable cost of the improvement. Of the following, the BEST justification for this procedure is that

    A. complete financial relief should be afforded to those landlords who upgrade their incinerators
    B. the number of tenants served by the incinerator is insufficient to award a rent increase
    C. part of the cost for reducing air pollution is spread among the general public, since all benefit from such reduction
    D. only those in the affected buildings should bear a cost increase

23. According to the rent and eviction regulations, the one of the following factors which shall be considered in deciding whether an offered accommodation for relocation is suitable is that

    A. it is reasonably accessible to the tenant's place of business and generally not less desirable in regard to community and commercial facilities than the former area
    B. the annual rental is not more than 20% of the tenant's annual income
    C. the building is in an area approved as a site for urban renewal or neighborhood conservation
    D. the accommodations are superior to comparable accommodations in public housing

24. According to the rent and eviction regulations, the one of the following which is a ground for eviction proceedings without a certificate from the city rent agency is that the

    A. landlord wishes to demolish the accommodation for the purpose of a building containing 20% more housing accommodations consisting of self-contained family units
    B. tenant is committing or permitting a nuisance or is maliciously or by reason of gross negligence substantially damaging the housing accommodations
    C. landlord wishes to substantially alter or remodel the premises for the purpose of subdividing an under-occupied housing accommodation
    D. tenant is not using the premises for his dwelling, and the occupants of the housing accomodations are sub-tenants who occupied under a rental agreement with the tenant

25. Nothing in the rent and eviction regulations shall be construed to require any person to offer any housing accomodations for rent.
    However, rent controlled housing accomodations already on the rental market may be withdrawn ONLY

    A. when tenants, other than those on a month-to-month basis, have refused to renew their leases or have been unable to reach agreement with the landlord on the terms of new leases
    B. after tenants have reached agreement with the landlord on stipends for moving and reimbursement for the rental difference for the period of the un-expired portion of their leases and their new apartments
    C. when relocation of the tenants has been accomplished on a voluntary basis and the building is completely empty
    D. after an order issued by the city rent agency under the regulations, if such withdrawal requires that a tenant be evicted

26. A landlord has painted a particular apartment on a three-year basis since the freeze date. The tenant now demands that the landlord paint her apartment on a two-year basis. The tenant applies for a reduction in rent for failure in service.
    The district rent office must

    A. issue an order decreasing the rent where the landlord refuses to paint every two years
    B. deny the application upon the landlord's proof of a three-year practice
    C. certify that a two-year practice exists in relation to this apartment
    D. delay final action pending certification of violations by the department of buildings

27. A tenant, at her own expense, has wallpapered the rooms of her apartment. She now demands periodic painting which is due. The landlord has refused and she has filed for a rent reduction.
    Given these facts, the one of the following which is TRUE is that the landlord

    A. can refuse to paint the apartment unless the tenant first removes the wallpaper
    B. can refuse to paint until the tenant moves her furniture to the middle of the room
    C. must replace the wallpaper with new paper because that is what is on the walls now
    D. cannot refuse to paint when the painting is due

28. Under the rent law, a landlord may be permitted recoupment of increase labor costs ONLY if

    A. the tenants are willing to share in the additional expense
    B. he has incurred increased labor costs and makes proper application for rental adjustments
    C. he enters into a labor agreement with a duly recognized union
    D. he can establish that the total residential rent income of the property is insufficient to absorb increased operating costs

29. A lease agreement providing for a rent increase for a controlled apartment may be executed for a term

    A. not exceeding 2 years
    B. of not less than 1 year
    C. of not less than 2 years
    D. of any length agreed upon by the parties

30. The conversion of a rent-controlled building to a cooperative requires full disclosure to tenants in a prospectus containing the details of the offering.
    The government official who is responsible for assuring such disclosure is the

    A. state attorney general
    B. chairman of the urban development corporation
    C. city corporation counsel
    D. secretary of housing and urban development

KEY (CORRECT ANSWERS)

1.	D	16.	D
2.	B	17.	C
3.	B	18.	C
4.	D	19.	B
5.	A	20.	C
6.	A	21.	A
7.	A	22.	C
8.	C	23.	A
9.	B	24.	B
10.	C	25.	D
11.	D	26.	B
12.	A	27.	A
13.	B	28.	B
14.	C	29.	C
15.	A	30.	A

EXAMINATION SECTION
TEST 1

DIRECTIONS: Each question or incomplete statement is followed by several suggested answers or completions. Select the one that BEST answers the question or completes the statement. *PRINT THE LETTER OF THE CORRECT ANSWER IN THE SPACE AT THE RIGHT.*

1. In a properly wired electrical circuit, the neutral wire is ALWAYS

    A. black or blue
    B. red or purple
    C. white or gray
    D. yellow or orange

    1.____

2. A circuit breaker is a safety device in an electrical system and can BEST be described as performing the same function as a

    A. fuse
    B. limit switch
    C. relay
    D. thermostat

    2.____

3. Which of the following is a difference between A.C. and D.C. electrical current?

    A. Ampere   B. Cycle   C. Volt   D. Watt

    3.____

4. Among the most common faults in providing electrical services is the furnishing of an inadequate number of outlets.
Such a condition will LEAST likely result in

    A. higher bills for electricity
    B. hazardous use of extension wiring
    C. overheating of wires
    D. overloaded circuits

    4.____

5. The force at which electricity is delivered is similar to pressure in a water supply system and is called

    A. amperage   B. current   C. wattage   D. voltage

    5.____

6. Which one of the following is NOT a general classification of windows?

    A. Awning   B. Casement   C. Sliding   D. Expanding

    6.____

7. All of the following are parts of a double-hung window EXCEPT the

    A. muntin   B. saddle   C. stile   D. rail

    7.____

8. Wooden obstructions placed between studs or floor joists to prevent fire from spreading in these natural flue spaces are called

    A. fire blocks
    B. fire walls
    C. fire stops
    D. flue dampers

    8.____

9. Plaster is a mixture GENERALLY consisting of water, sand, and

    A. concrete
    B. gypsum
    C. aggregate
    D. calcium chloride

    9.____

10. A parapet wall is that part of the masonry that extends above the roofline and is capped with noncombustible material.
    Of the following, one purpose a parapet wall does NOT serve is to

    A. strengthen the wall
    B. prevent people from falling off the roof
    C. prevent spread of fire
    D. provide a rest for fire department ladders

11. Large quantity purchasers of supplies and equipment often make their purchases on the basis of specifications. Which one of the following is NOT a good reason for using specifications?
    Specifications

    A. often offer a good description of what a product can do
    B. enable price comparisons since they set forth the price range to be paid for products
    C. set forth minimum standards that a product should meet
    D. enable the purchase of standardized products

12. The MAXIMUM permissible height of fences in residential districts in the city is _____ feet.

    A. 12   B. 10   C. 8   D. 6

13. A real estate manager under your supervision tells you that he is annoyed with some of his tenants who tend to lose their keys and then annoy the staff with requests for assistance.
    Which of the following suggestions should NOT be made to such tenants?

    A. Keep a duplicate set of keys at place of employment.
    B. Leave a duplicate set of keys with a friend or a relative.
    C. Put keys on a ring with name and address for prompt return if lost.
    D. Secure keys more firmly to the person by using a key chain or necklace.

14. An auxiliary lock is the simplest device to bolster the security offered by a primary door lock.
    Of the following, the STRONGEST type of auxiliary lock is usually the

    A. key-in-the-knob   B. thimble-groove
    C. trigger-bolt   D. vertical-bolt

15. In a multiple dwelling of nine or more dwelling units, where janitorial services are NOT performed on an approved 24-hour-a-day basis, the janitor MUST

    A. attend an approved course of instruction in the operation of low pressure boilers within three days of employment
    B. reside in or within a distance of one block or 200 feet, unless the owner resides in the multiple dwelling
    C. be licensed to operated low pressure boilers or have received a temporary permit therefor
    D. be a resident of the building or of an immediately adjoining building if the two buildings are under the same ownership

16. The Multiple Dwelling Law permits the installation of a window security gate on a fire escape window.
In order to be acceptable in the city, the gate has to be stamped with a number indicating the approval of the Board of Standards and Appeals, should NOT require the use of a padlock, and MUST be

    A. openable from the inside without the use of a key
    B. constructed with a galvanized or other rust-proof finish
    C. connected to a sufficiently audible alarm device
    D. of the collapsible *accordion* type

17. A tenant tells you that she wishes to install a food waste disposer in her kitchen sink. You should inform her that

    A. such disposers are forbidden in the city because the sewage system cannot handle the additional waste load
    B. she is free to do so, provided the installation is done by a licensed plumber
    C. you will have the plumbing examined by a building inspector to make sure it is adequate in size
    D. within seven days after installation she must present to you a Certificate of Major Appliance Installation, duly notarized

18. When installing a new lighting fixture to replace an old one which is located in an outlet box, all of the following are safety precautions EXCEPT

    A. turning off the wall switch
    B. removing the fuse
    C. opening the circuit breaker
    D. replacing the bulb

19. During the heating season, landlords are required to maintain a minimum indoor temperature of 68° F. during the hours between 6 A.M. and 10 P.M. when the outdoor temperature falls below the allowable minimum temperature of

    A. 40° F   B. 45° F   C. 50° F   D. 55° F

20. When outside temperatures fall below certain levels, landlords are required to provide heat during the period from

    A. October 1 to April 30
    B. October 1 to May 31
    C. November 1 to April 30
    D. November 1 to May 31

21. In the city, many buildings have water tanks on the roof for all of the following reasons EXCEPT to

    A. furnish water for human consumption
    B. provide a water reserve for firefighting
    C. reduce stagnation in the water supply
    D. assure water pressure on the upper floors

22. A real estate manager was asked for his opinion on the purchase of a glass cutter. He recommended a steel wheel model rather than one with a carbide wheel.
His advice was

   A. *poor;* mainly because the steel wheel is apt to cause the glass to splinter or break when it is used
   B. *good;* mainly because the steel wheel is less expensive
   C. *good;* mainly because the carbide wheel puts a sharper edge on the glass
   D. *poor;* mainly because the steel wheel is not all-purpose

23. Which of the following is GENERALLY an advantage of using alkyd paint rather than latex paint?
It

   A. has better hiding power
   B. dries faster
   C. is easier to apply
   D. has less odor

24. In accordance with the Housing Maintenance Code, the central heating system of a multiple dwelling MUST be inspected by a qualified person at least

   A. in alternate years B. annually
   C. semi-annually D. quarterly

25. In accordance with the Housing Maintenance Code, hot water MUST generally be provided to tenants in a multiple dwelling between the hours of

   A. 5 A.M. and 10 P.M.
   B. 5 A.M. and 11 P.M.
   C. 6 A.M. and 9 P.M.
   D. 6 A.M. and Midnight

KEY (CORRECT ANSWERS)

1.	C		11.	B
2.	A		12.	D
3.	B		13.	C
4.	A		14.	D
5.	D		15.	B
6.	D		16.	A
7.	B		17.	A
8.	C		18.	D
9.	B		19.	D
10.	A		20.	B

21. C
22. B
23. A
24. B
25. D

TEST 2

DIRECTIONS: Each question or incomplete statement is followed by several suggested answers or completions. Select the one that BEST answers the question or completes the statement. *PRINT THE LETTER OF THE CORRECT ANSWER IN THE SPACE AT THE RIGHT.*

1. A tenant with whom you have dealt in the past comes to you with a question about general departmental policy. The tenant gives no reason for seeking this information. Of the following, the BEST way of dealing with him would usually be to

    A. answer his question and state the basis for the policy
    B. refrain from answering the question until he reveals his reason for asking it
    C. tell him that you cannot give him information for which he has no need
    D. withhold the information until you have discussed the matter with your superior

    1.____

2. Notices or advertisements to sell real estate that contain the *seven basic facts* on properties usually bring better results.
   Of the following, which of these facts is considered LEAST important?

    A. Design
    B. Location
    C. Number of rooms
    D. Price and terms

    2.____

3. According to the Sternlieb report (THE URBAN HOUSING DILEMMA: THE DYNAMICS OF NEW YORK CITY'S RENT CONTROLLED HOUSING), it was found that

    A. area disadvantages would not interfere with the availability of financing if rent control were removed
    B. the abolition of rent control would provide a solution to local housing problems, based on studies of other cities
    C. most of the low rent, rent-controlled buildings are owned by persons who own only one, or at most two, other buildings
    D. the income levels of rent-controlled buildings have made it impossible to maintain any of these buildings properly

    3.____

4. A squatter is MOST NEARLY a tenant

    A. in fee simple   B. by the entirety
    C. in common   D. at sufferance

    4.____

5. The new fire safety code for high-rise office buildings was the outcome of a study started after five persons died in high-rise fires.
   This code requires

    A. acquisition of additional fire damage and loss insurance wherever coverage is inadequate for full indemnification
    B. installation of devices to prevent automatic elevators from being drawn to floors where there is a fire
    C. installation of automatic sprinkler systems using foaming fire-extinguishing chemicals rather than water
    D. replacement of non-opening windows with removable panels offering ready access for firemen

    5.____

6. With the increase in housing problems in the city, some tenant organizations have advocated and led rent strikes. Of the following, the BASIC reason for rent strikes is that the tenants involved

   A. want to force landlords to improve conditions in the buildings
   B. want court permission to withhold rent under the Real Property Actions and Proceedings Law
   C. have been encouraged to greater activism by the Legal Aid Society
   D. are already faced with dispossess action and have little to lose

7. A recent study by the city planning commission states that the MAIN reason that industries and business firms consider leaving the city is

   A. a lack of dependable employees
   B. their need for more space for expansion
   C. labor union disputes and high wages
   D. the increasing crime rate

8. The city's rent control law provides that certain *heads of households* over age 62 can

   A. be exempted from rent increase by filing for a rent exemption certificate
   B. receive exemption from decontrol provided they have custody of three or more minor children
   C. request and receive rent reductions if they agree to perform simple janitorial duties
   D. transfer possession of the premises to any person, and for any agreed-upon consideration

9. A person who, after the end of the term of a lease, retains possession as tenant of the property leased, is known as a

   A. freehold   B. holder in due course
   C. hold over   D. leasehold

10. When used in connection with fire or vandalism insurance, the term *deductible* refers to

    A. an amount that is noncompensable
    B. coverage sold through a pool
    C. optional modification of terms
    D. the full value of the loss

11. Tenants entering long-term leases for office space often rent more space than they need immediately in order to provide for future needs.
    With respect to such unused space, the USUAL practice of such tenants is to

    A. renegotiate the lease   B. seek a reduction
    C. sublet the space   D. delay expansion

12. The practice of temporarily relocating tenants into other housing within the same urban renewal area is USUALLY known as

    A. parceling   B. onsiting
    C. recycling   D. rotating

13. In the city, special zoning district regulations are used to control commercial real estate development in certain area locations.
    In these districts, developers are permitted density bonuses if they

    A. provide plazas and other specified public amenities
    B. construct non-subsidized housing
    C. increase the total density through additional height
    D. consolidate non-contiguous plots

14. The Federal Housing Administration has, in recent years, become a major landlord.
    The BASIC reason for this is that

    A. the Federal Housing Administration is operating low income leased housing programs
    B. major cities where housing is rapidly decaying have housing programs which are under exclusive Federal control
    C. the Federal Housing Administration has recently purchased depressed properties for possible future site use
    D. real estate speculators have sold many overpriced and defective homes whose mortgages were guaranteed and subsequently foreclosed by the Federal Housing Administration

15. Recently, it has been suggested that new housing, industrial, and recreational facilities be built on unused areas of the city's waterfront.
    Of the following, the MAJOR obstacle to carrying out this proposal is

    A. a shortage of containerization facilities
    B. the difficulty in relocating displaced tenants
    C. the current overuse of the piers
    D. a lack of available financial support

16. A legal requirement that there be conspicuous notice provided to tenants in connection with the posting of notices would mean MOST NEARLY that the notice be

    A. posted by an employee in a conspicuous place
    B. posted in a place which is reasonably calculated to impart the information
    C. distributed so that each tenant receives a copy
    D. written in simplified English rather than the usual legalistic terminology

17. The city Board of Standards and Appeals determines appeals from certain administrative decisions of a number of city agencies.
    The one of the following agencies whose decisions are NOT subject to review by the aforementioned Board is the

    A. Department of Buildings
    B. Department of Ports and Terminals
    C. Department of Tax Collection
    D. Fire Department

18. Single-room occupants, usually poor, elderly and unemployable, have become an increasingly large problem in the city because of the steadily shrinking stock of single-room occupancy buildings.
    The MAJOR reason for this decrease is that

    A. improved code enforcement by several city agencies has resulted in the shutting down of these unsafe buildings
    B. many single-room dwellings have been converted into small high-rental apartments or demolished under urban renewal
    C. much of this housing has been abandoned by owners who cannot, or will not, pay the taxes that have become due
    D. the demand for single rooms has been increased by an influx of single persons from other parts of the United States

19. Which of the following statements about the assessed valuation of real property in the city is MOST NEARLY correct?

    A. Each county determines rates for its jurisdiction.
    B. It has a relationship to the city's debt limit.
    C. It is generally considered to produce only minor revenue.
    D. Proposed changes are subject to a community referendum.

20. A Certificate of Eviction for a residential building erected prior to January 1, 1982 is USUALLY issued by the

    A. Department of Real Property Assessment
    B. Department of Relocation and Management Services
    C. Department of Rent and Housing Maintenance
    D. City Planning Commission

21. *In rem* buildings become the property of the city because of

    A. tax delinquency   B. condemnation
    C. public improvement   D. eminent domain

22. A non-profit membership corporation empowered to provide various services, including the improvement, development, repair, management, maintenance, and operation of real property acquired by the city in connection with urban renewal projects, is known as the

    A. City Urban Development Operations Corporation
    B. City Urban Renewal Management Corporation
    C. Urban Relocation Corporation
    D. Urban Resources Corporation

23. The designations *landmark* and *historic district,* when approved by the Landmarks Preservation Commission and ratified by the Board of Estimate, mean that

    A. exterior alterations to buildings cannot be made without prior approval of the Commission
    B. the Comptroller and Director of the Budget must agree jointly to the payment of city funds for improvements
    C. the premises must be open at reasonable times to guided tours conducted by the Commission
    D. neither exterior nor interior alterations may be made in any circumstances

24. The New York Plan is an agreement which involves the state, the city, and the building and construction industry.
Its MAIN purpose is to

    A. expedite the relocation of persons displaced by capital construction projects
    B. increase the dollar amount of non-residential building construction
    C. provide training and employment for minority group members
    D. reduce the amount of housing abandonment and subsequent receiverships

25. The State Labor Law provides that workers on any publicly assisted contract construction site MUST

    A. be paid the prevailing wages for their respective trades
    B. be members of a union approved by the Attorney General
    C. have completed a formal apprenticeship program
    D. receive wages for at least 215 days each year

Questions 26-35.

DIRECTIONS: Questions 26 through 35 are to be answered on the basis of the following tables, which contain data concerning the Green Valley Region, a fictional area.

HOUSING PATTERNS, GREEN VALLEY REGION 1990-2000

TABLE I

TYPE OF HOUSING	SUBURBS		TOWNS		REGION TOTAL*	
	1990	2000	1990	2000	1990	2000
Multi-Unit Dwellings	2,600	5,200	9,300	10,900	13,700	18,800
Single-Unit Dwellings	15,100	17,700	11,000	11,400	43,700	46,900
Mobile Dwellings	300	?	900	1,800	14,700	31,400
TOTAL	18,000	23,600	21,200	24,100	72,100	97,100

*NOTE: Region totals include other categories in addition to suburbs and towns.

TABLE II
SUBSTANDARD HOUSING, GREEN VALLEY REGION
(INCLUDED IN FIGURES IN TABLE I, ABOVE)

	1990-800 UNITS	2000-1,200 UNITS
Multi-Unit	64%	54%
Single-Unit	33%	28%
Mobile	3%	18%

26. If the single-unit dwellings in towns in 1990 each contained an average of 5.1 rooms, the total number of rooms in this category was MOST NEARLY

    A. 56,000   B. 61,000   C. 561,000   D. 651,000

27. The number of mobile dwellings in the suburbs in 2000 was

    A. 500   B. 600   C. 700   D. 800

28. From 1990 to 2000, the total number of all Green Valley Region housing units increased by MOST NEARLY 28._____

    A. 31%   B. 34%   C. 37%   D. 40%

29. For 2000, what was the TOTAL number of substandard multi-unit dwellings? 29._____

    A. 548   B. 573   C. 623   D. 648

30. In the towns, from 1990 to 2000, the type of housing having the LARGEST proportionate increase was 30._____

    A. mobile   B. multi-unit
    C. single-unit   D. substandard

31. In 2000, the TOTAL number of dwellings which were not substandard was 31._____

    A. 95,300   B. 95,900   C. 96,200   D. 96,500

32. Assume that, in 1990, 3.5 persons was the average occupancy in the towns in each kind of dwelling. 32._____
    Thus, the population of the towns in the Green Valley Region in 1990 was

    A. 73,600   B. 73,800   C. 74,000   D. 74,200

33. Which of the following statements concerning mobile dwellings is CORRECT? 33._____

    A. In 2000, mobile dwellings were the largest category of substandard dwellings.
    B. In 1990, the number of mobile dwellings in suburbs was greater by *30%* than the number in towns.
    C. In the Green Valley Region during the period 1990-2000, the number of mobile dwellings increased by 50%.
    D. In 1990, the total number of mobile dwellings in the Green Valley Region was less than 25% of the total number of all dwellings.

34. Assume that, of the single-unit dwellings not in suburbs and towns in 1990, 20% were in villages. 34._____
    Therefore, the number of single-unit dwellings in villages in 1990 was

    A. 2,480   B. 3,070   C. 3,520   D. 4,110

35. Assume that in the Green Valley Region, the following changes are expected in 2010 as compared to 2000: the number of suburban dwellings will increase by 30%; the number of town dwellings will decrease by 15%. Therefore, the ratio of suburban dwellings to town dwellings expected for 2010 is MOST NEARLY 35._____

    A. 3 to 2   B. 4 to 3   C. 5 to 4   D. 6 to 5

Questions 36-38.

DIRECTIONS: Questions 36 through 38 are to be answered on the basis of the following paragraph.

In recent years, new and important emphasis has been placed upon the maximum use of conservation and rehabilitation techniques in carrying out programs of urban renewal and revitalization. In urban renewal projects where existing structures are hopelessly deteriorated or land uses are incompatible with the community's overall plans, the entire area may be *acquired, cleared, and sold for redevelopment. However, where existing structures are basically sound but have deteriorated to the point where they are a <u>blighting</u> influence on the neighborhood, they may be salvaged through a program of rehabilitation and reconditioning.*

36. According to the above paragraph, the one of the following which is MOST likely to cause area-wide razing of the buildings in urban renewal programs is

    A. a program of rehabilitation and reconditioning
    B. concerted insistence by landlords and tenants that certain buildings be bulldozed
    C. an inability of community groups to agree on priorities for staged clearance
    D. land use contrary to the community's general plan

37. According to the above paragraph, rehabilitation of structures may take place if

    A. new conservation and rehabilitation techniques are used
    B. salvaging all the buildings in the entire area is hopeless
    C. the community wishes to preserve historic structures
    D. the existing buildings are structurally sound

38. As used in the above paragraph, the word *blighting* means MOST NEARLY

    A. ruining   B. infrequent
    C. recurrent   D. traditional

Questions 39-42.

DIRECTIONS: Questions 39 through 42 are to be answered SOLELY on the basis of the following paragraph.

The concentration of publicly assisted housing in central cities -- because the suburbs do not want them and effectively bar them -- is usually <u>rationalized</u> by a solicitous regard for keeping intact the city neighborhoods cherished by low-income groups. If one accepted this as valid, the devotion of minorities to blighted city neighborhoods in preference to suburban employment and housing would be an historic first. Certainly no such devotion was visible among the millions who have deserted their city neighborhoods in the last 25 years even if it meant an arduous daily trip from the suburbs to their jobs in the cities.

39. The writer implies that MOST poor people

    A. prefer isolation   B. fear change
    C. are angry   D. seek betterment

40. The general tone of the paragraph is BEST characterized as

    A. uncertain   B. skeptical
    C. evasive   D. indifferent

41. As used in the above paragraph, the word *rationalize* means MOST NEARLY

    A. dispute   B. justify   C. deny   D. locate

42. According to the above paragraph, publicly assisted housing is concentrated in the central cities PRIMARILY because

    A. city dwellers are unable to find satisfactory housing
    B. deterioration of older housing has increased in recent years
    C. suburbanites have opposed the movement of the poor to the suburbs
    D. employment opportunities have decreased in the suburbs

Questions 43-46.

DIRECTIONS: Questions 43 through 46 are to be answered SOLELY on the basis of the following paragraph.

A city may expand by growing vertically through the replacement of lower buildings with higher ones; or by filling in open spaces between settled areas; or by extending the existing settled area. When the settled area is expanded, growth may take several forms, the most important forms being concentric circle or ring growth around the central nucleus; axial growth, with prongs or finger-like extensions moving out along main transportation routes; and suburban growth, with the establishment of islands of settlements before the expansion of the main city area. These types of expansion are characteristic of most large cities. Baltimore was for a long time a good example of ring growth, whereas New York, Chicago, and Detroit illustrate axial and suburban growth.

43. The title that BEST expresses the theme of this paragraph is

    A. FORMS OF CITY EXPANSION
    B. MAJOR METROPOLITAN PROBLEMS
    C. METHODS OF URBAN PLANNING
    D. SUBURBAN GROWTH IN AMERICA

44. The one of the following which is example of vertical growth is the

    A. settlement of year-round residents along the upper Hudson River
    B. restoration of former rooming houses to their original brownstone condition
    C. subdivision of large estates into small lot semidetached houses
    D. erection of the World Trade Center in New York City

45. A city that grew as a concentric circle is

    A. Baltimore   B. New York   C. Chicago   D. Detroit

46. When the author speaks of axial growth, he refers to a situation where

    A. expansion is primarily into rural areas until suburbs are thereby created
    B. small towns and villages are consolidated by gradually growing until one large city is created
    C. the direction in which a city expands is determined by the location of major highways
    D. the number of new buildings is greater than the number of old buildings demolished

Questions 47-50.

DIRECTIONS: Questions 47 through 50 are to be answered SOLELY on the basis of the following paragraph.

Although the suburbs have provided housing and employment for millions of additional families since 1970, many suburban communities have maintained controls over the kinds of families who can live in them. Suburban attitudes have been formed by reaction against a perception of crowded, harassed city life and threatening alien city people. As population, taxable income, and jobs have left the cities for the suburbs, the "urban crisis" of substandard housing, declining levels of education and public services, and decreasing employment opportunities has been created. The crisis, however, is not urban at all, but national, and in part a result of the suburban policy that discourages outward movement by the urban poor.

47. According to the above paragraph, the quality of urban life

    A. is determined by public opinion in the cities
    B. has worsened in recent years
    C. is similar to rural life
    D. can be changed by political means

48. According to the above paragraph, suburban communities have

    A. tried to show that the urban crisis is really a national crisis
    B. avoided taking a position on the urban crisis
    C. been involved in causing the urban crisis
    D. been the innocent victims of the urban crisis

49. According to the above paragraph, the poor have

    A. become increasingly sophisticated in their attempts to move to the suburbs
    B. generally been excluded from the suburbs
    C. lost incentive for betterment of their living conditions
    D. sought improvement of the central cities

50. As used in the above paragraph, the word *perception* means MOST NEARLY

    A. development   B. impression
    C. opposition   D. uncertainty

KEY (CORRECT ANSWERS)

1. A	11. C	21. A	31. B	41. B
2. A	12. B	22. B	32. D	42. D
3. C	13. A	23. A	33. D	43. A
4. D	14. D	24. C	34. C	44. D
5. B	15. D	25. A	35. A	45. A
6. A	16. B	26. A	36. D	46. C
7. B	17. C	27. C	37. D	47. B
8. A	18. B	28. B	38. A	48. C
9. C	19. B	29. D	39. D	49. B
10. A	20. C	30. A	40. B	50. B

TEST 3

DIRECTIONS: Each question or incomplete statement is followed by several suggested answers or completions. Select the one that BEST answers the question or completes the statement. *PRINT THE LETTER OF THE CORRECT ANSWER IN THE SPACE AT THE RIGHT.*

1. In awarding contracts for maintenance repair work, the MOST important rule to follow is to 1.____

   A. judge on competitive bidding, based on written specifications
   B. prequalify the bidders, based only on length of time in business
   C. require bidding and payment bonds from all bidders
   D. require performance bonds from all bidders

2. Which one of the following methods is MOST effective for monitoring the performance of large maintenance contracts? 2.____

   A. Establishing a percentage retainer as work is completed by submittal of invoices.
   B. Having contractor attest to amount of work performed.
   C. Requiring performance bonds and placing responsibility on bonding company.
   D. Spot-checking of work, performed by inspectors who are rotated.

3. The one of the following that MOST frequently occurs when a plug fuse blows is that the 3.____

   A. isinglass window melts
   B. mica window cracks
   C. window of the fuse blackens
   D. window of the fuse turns blue

4. If 20-ampere fuses in a 20-ampere circuit in an electric lighting panel repeatedly blow out, the BEST action to take is t 4.____

   A. install a ground fault interrupter
   B. install a fuse having a higher ampere rating
   C. trouble-shoot the circuit before replacing the fuse
   D. replace the fuse with a solid copper bar

5. One of the BASIC parts of a stairway is the 5.____

   A. apron   B. soffit   C. stool   D. threshold

6. A plumbing trap is a device used in a waste system to 6.____

   A. facilitate the waste discharge from plumbing fixtures
   B. limit the discharge of waste
   C. prevent backflow to a water main
   D. prevent the passage of sewer gas into the building

7. Gas-fueled or electric space or water heaters, where permitted by law in a multiple dwelling, are required to
    A. be installed by the owner according to the wishes of the tenant as to capacity, number, and location
    B. furnish the same standard of heat or hot water supply as is required to be furnished from a central heat or hot water system
    C. be operated so that the owner of the building is solely responsible for the full cost of the gas or electricity used by such heaters
    D. be repaired and maintained by the tenant with no charge or liability to the landlord or his agent

7.____

8. At what point is the water supply system to a building USUALLY shut off by a municipality?
   At the
    A. house wall   B. corporation cock
    C. house basement   D. meter

8.____

9. A float and thermostat trap is a part of which of the following piping systems? _____ system.
    A. Cold water   B. Hot water
    C. Steam heating   D. Waste line

9.____

10. Air chambers are built into plumbing systems to
    A. decrease water flow
    B. filter out water-borne sand
    C. inhibit rust formation
    D. reduce water hammer

10.____

11. On which type of heating system is a plenum chamber used?
    A. Hot air   B. Hot water
    C. One-pipe steam   D. Two-pipe steam

11.____

12. Heating boilers may be classified according to several kinds of characteristics. All of the following are types of boilers EXCEPT
    A. radiator   B. Scotch marine
    C. sectional   D. water-tube

12.____

13. In a large multiple dwelling, under properly controlled maintenance conditions, it would be BEST to use fuel oil which is classified as grade number
    A. 2   B. 3   C. 4   D. 6

13.____

14. For proper service, vapor barriers used in roofs and exterior walls of buildings should NOT be made of
    A. asphalted paper   B. canvas
    C. metal foil   D. plastic

14.____

15. According to the housing maintenance code, in a room located on the top story of a converted dwelling, a skylight

    A. of the proper dimensions may be substituted for a required window
    B. is not permissible except in fire-proof buildings
    C. is allowable as a means of emergency exit in lieu of a fire escape provided an adequate ladder is installed
    D. is forbidden in all dwelling units

16. Provisions for non-conforming uses put into zoning ordinances ordinarily prohibit all of the following EXCEPT the

    A. enlargement or expansion of a non-conforming use
    B. changing the non-conforming use to any other non-conforming use
    C. continuance of an established non-conforming use
    D. complete reconstruction of the non-conforming use

17. Permission to do some act contrary to a zoning ordinance is known as a(n)

    A. encroachment   B. indenture
    C. ordinance   D. variance

18. The custodian of a group of buildings had, in his office, a large pegboard which holds duplicate keys for all his tenants. He tagged the keys with coded numbers instead of the actual apartment designations.
    The use of coded keys is USUALLY considered to be

    A. *good;* it allows keys to be more quickly located
    B. *good;* it reduces the danger of misuse of keys
    C. *bad;* it requires an additional cost in handling keys
    D. *bad;* tenants will be unable to recognize their keys

19. Until recently, it was unlawful to have bars or gates on a fire escape window.
    Now, the law permits the installation of a security gate or device, provided that it has stamped on it a Board of Standards and Appeals number and it

    A. uses only an approved padlock which can be opened only from the inside with the use of a key
    B. does not require any type of padlock and can be opened from the inside with the use of a key
    C. uses only an approved padlock which can be opened from either side with the use of a key
    D. does not require any type of padlock and can be opened from the inside without the use of a key

20. Mortise locks provide more security than key-in-the-knob locks because MOST of the locking mechanism of a mortise lock is

    A. accessible from outside the door
    B. enclosed in the beveled convenience latch
    C. located in a metal enclosure in the door, rather than in the knob
    D. removable for adjustment and repair

21. A tenant installed on his door a special lock of the double cylinder type. This type of lock can be locked with a key from the inside.
The major DISADVANTAGE of such a lock is that

    A. a skillful burglar would be able to open it more quickly
    B. in a fire or other emergency a key may not be available to open the door from the inside
    C. it is a violation of both state and city laws and regulations
    D. when repairs are necessary, access to the inside cylinder is difficult

21.____

22. It is generally agreed that the BEST protection for most kinds of buildings against prowlers and thieves is provided by

    A. a bell, buzzer, and voice intercommunication system
    B. a well-trained security and maintenance staff
    C. closed-circuit television and convex mirrors
    D. locks of some kind on all doors

22.____

23. During the heating season, landlords are required to maintain a minimum indoor temperature of 55° F. during the hours between 10 P.M. to 6 A.M., when the outdoor temperature falls below the allowable minimum point of

    A. 30° F. B. 35° F. C. 40° F. D. 45° F.

23.____

24. According to the BEST practice, a minor change in a lease between landlord and tenant

    A. should be agreed to orally provided that a witness is present
    B. must have a special form which should be securely affixed to the original lease
    C. should be put in writing as part of the lease and signed by both parties
    D. should not be made unless the circumstances are exceptional since such changes require court approval

24.____

25. Housing units that are completely finished at a factory, including installation of wiring, plumbing, and carpeting, and are usually ready for occupancy except for major utilities, are known as _____ units.

    A. cluster   B. modular
    C. intrinsic   D. quadplex

25.____

26. The owner of a multiple dwelling must paint every fire escape with two coats of paint in contrasting colors. The requirement that two colors be used

    A. is based on the fact that two colors will provide greater protection to the metal
    B. facilitates scraping and removal of the paint after the mandatory period of five years
    C. is for the purpose of combining the first color with the second color to provide a neutral tone
    D. allows for inspection and verification that two coats of paint were actually used

26.____

27. The term *key money* refers to

   A. so-called *seed money* used to reduce the amount of money borrowed to finance residential construction
   B. the difference between the controlled rent for a given apartment and the rent such an apartment would bring if uncontrolled
   C. the *fee,* or bribe, demanded of a prospective tenant by someone in a position to provide an apartment
   D. cooperative maintenance charges which are at a level that middle-income families can afford

28. The principle of independence of covenants rather than interdependence of covenants applies to a landlord-tenant lease, according to real property law.
    The effect of this independence of covenants is that NEARLY ALWAYS

   A. the tenant is required to consult an attorney prior to entering into a long-term lease
   B. the tenant must continue to pay rent even if customary services are interrupted
   C. landlords are placed under great pressure to modify lease terms even after they have been agreed to
   D. landlords will ask tenants to sign a statement reading *I solemnly affirm that I have read and fully understand the terms of this lease*

29. A condition which is inserted in a deed, lease, mortgage, or contract, and on the performance or non-performance of which the validity of the instrument USUALLY depends, is known as a

   A. pendency
   B. prima facie
   C. pro tempore
   D. proviso

30. A landlord, without intent to oust a tenant, commits an act which deprives the tenant of the beneficial enjoyment of the premises, and the tenant voluntarily gives up possession. Such a situation is known as

   A. destructive conversion
   B. homestead exemption
   C. constructive eviction
   D. due reversion

31. The term *class action,* used in a lawsuit brought against a landlord, means MOST NEARLY that the lawsuit is an action brought on behalf of

   A. a low-income economic group
   B. an ethnic minority group
   C. elderly rent-controlled tenants
   D. persons similarly situated

32. In a public or private housing development which has admission rules concerning income level, the amount above the basic rent that must be paid by a tenant whose income rises above such level is USUALLY known as a

   A. balance
   B. net overage
   C. surcharge
   D. voluntary assessment

33. The one of the following which is USUALLY included in a standard residential lease is

    A. a description of premises
    B. a guarantee of habitability
    C. the right to deduct repair costs
    D. a 90-day right to cancel

34. Assume that a landlord, wishing to stop a tenant from committing a nuisance on the landlord's property, seeks a court order.
    The court order would GENERALLY be referred to as a(n)

    A. injunction
    B. writ of mandamus
    C. real estate estoppel
    D. tenant referral

35. State legislation prohibits real estate brokers from using racial considerations to frighten homeowners into selling.
    Nevertheless, city officials have urged the passage of even stricter legislation against such *blockbusting* MAINLY because, as matters now stand,

    A. brokers can still break up neighborhoods by warning of declining property values, without specifically referring to any minority group
    B. real estate associations are united in their support of blockbusting tactics
    C. homeowners are fearful of reporting instances of blockbusting due to the severe penalties of the law for conspiring with blockbusters
    D. fraudulent unsworn testimony is freely accepted at public hearings without any penalties for false statements, since testimony need not be sworn to

36. Use and occupancy insurance is insurance that protects against loss of

    A. gross receipts following an unprovoked termination of lease
    B. net income resulting from condemnation
    C. rent resulting from destruction of a building
    D. things substantial and immovable

37. The MAIN advantage for the purchaser of real estate title insurance is that such insurance generally

    A. guarantees that the terms of mortgage agreements will be complied with
    B. pays for damages resulting from defects in title
    C. guarantees that no restrictions will be placed upon property in the future
    D. guarantees that the insurer will take title to the property in the event of hidden defects

38. An IMPORTANT advantage of building attached homes with common party walls is that

    A. construction of this type encourages long-term tenancy
    B. higher land costs can be supported
    C. occupants are less likely to make demands on owners or real estate managers
    D. such homes are particularly resistive to the spread of fire

39. Guidelines designed to end sex discrimination in employment were recently issued by the city government for the information of contractors doing business with the city. These guidelines call on contractors to do all of the following EXCEPT to

    A. abolish all job duties that require extraordinary physical strength
    B. base qualifications for employment solely on ability or performance
    C. eliminate from employment applications questions about marital or parental status
    D. remove sex-based restrictive titles from job descriptions

40. The U.S. Department of Housing and Urban Development has set up a direct-dial, toll-free Washington telephone number of public use in reporting housing discrimination. Which of the following statements states the reason given by the Department of Housing and Urban Development?

    A. Although housing discrimination has generally been eliminated, and most persons know how to secure their rights, vigilance is always necessary.
    B. Housing discrimination continues, primarily because many persons do not know about the law, nor do they know how and where to report if they meet discrimination.
    C. Irrespective of the existence or non-existence of housing discrimination, a public relations program should be based upon image.
    D. Whether housing discrimination is or is not illusory, a certain segment of society will always require solicitous and understanding treatment.

41. The number of rent-stabilized apartments in the city is _____ the number of rent-controlled apartments.

    A. based on a fixed ratio to
    B. about the same as
    C. greater than
    D. less than

42. The court which has landlord and tenant parts is the

    A. Civil Court
    B. Court of Appeals
    C. Criminal Court
    D. Family Court

43. A city Mitchell-Lama rental development received tax and mortgage benefits from the city.
    However, as a requirement for obtaining such benefits, the development had to

    A. join the city-wide tenants' council
    B. grant priority in admission to city residents
    C. make payments into the city's general fund
    D. allow strict city supervision and regulation, especially of rents

44. An organization that is privately owned but is subject to control by the Federal government, and which stimulates mortgage lending, is the

    A. Federal Housing Administration
    B. Federal National Mortgage Association
    C. Real Property Lending Association
    D. National Housing Mortgage Association

45. The present building code is different from the former code PRIMARILY in that, under the present code, building materials

    A. are listed in order according to degree of acceptability
    B. must meet standards developed by the Department of Purchase
    C. must meet specified performance test standards
    D. that will be developed in the future are to eliminate metal as far as possible

46. Appeals from real property tax assessments in the city are heard FIRST by the

    A. Board of Estimate
    B. Board of Standards and Appeals
    C. Budget Commission
    D. Tax Commission

47. The Rent Stabilization Law requires that at least 35% of the tenants of an eligible building agree to purchase their apartments before the building can be converted to a cooperative. Some critics, however, advocate raising the minimum number who must agree to 51%. They claim that the tenants would benefit.
    Of the following, the MAJOR benefit to the tenants is MOST likely to be that

    A. increasing the number of tenants consenting would provide more money to reduce monthly maintenance costs
    B. the owner's terms may be lower if he must bargain with more tenants
    C. the owner could more promptly complete the transaction since more cash would be available to him
    D. the sale would be more easily completed since the rest of the tenants would be more likely to join the majority consenting

48. In an R-10 zone, the city's highest residential density, 10 square feet of floor area is allowed for each square foot of land.
    In addition, a bonus of 20% is obtainable for

    A. maximum use of architectural metals
    B. keeping return on equity constant
    C. providing open plazas at street level
    D. buildings which are used by wholesalers

49. In the city, buildings with out-of-order water meters are not billed for water until meters are repaired.
    The result of such non-billing is that

    A. bills for estate taxes are held up
    B. no accurate knowledge of water use exists, with the result that a possible water shortage might not be promptly detected
    C. it can be advantageous for violators not to comply with official requests to repair meters since, in effect, they obtain interest-free loans from the city
    D. the water meter readers lack adequate and timely information about ownership and general classification of buildings

50. The recent public outcry against the use of asbestos in fire-proofing steel beams is based upon the fact that

   A. airborne asbestos particles cause slippery dust granules to settle over many parts of the city
   B. increasing construction costs could be significantly reduced by substituting other materials
   C. inhalation of asbestos is associated with an increased incidence of cancer
   D. water damage in skyscraper fires can be reduced by more effective means

KEY (CORRECT ANSWERS)

1. A	11. A	21. B	31. D	41. D
2. D	12. A	22. B	32. C	42. A
3. C	13. D	23. C	33. A	43. D
4. C	14. B	24. C	34. A	44. B
5. B	15. A	25. B	35. A	45. C
6. D	16. C	26. D	36. C	46. D
7. B	17. D	27. C	37. B	47. B
8. B	18. B	28. B	38. B	48. C
9. C	19. D	29. D	39. A	49. C
10. D	20. C	30. C	40. B	50. C

EXAMINATION SECTION
TEST 1

DIRECTIONS: Each question or incomplete statement is followed by several suggested answers or completions. Select the one that BEST answers the question or completes the statement. *PRINT THE LETTER OF THE CORRECT ANSWER IN THE SPACE AT THE RIGHT.*

1. At an interview, a tenant who is late in rent payment explains that the delay was due to a temporary reduction in the family income. You notice, however, that her clothing appears new and expensive.
   Of the following, the MOST advisable action to take is to
   A. accept her explanation of rent payment delay but warn her that rent payments must be made on time
   B. ascertain if the family income is being mismanaged
   C. compliment her on the excellence of her appearance while accepting her explanation of delay in payment of rent
   D. offer to assist the tenant in preparing a budget
   E. point out tactfully to the tenant the apparent discrepancy between her appearance and her statement

   1.____

2. A housing assistant observes a boy just beginning to cut his initials in a wood slat on a bench. When spoken to, the boy says that he does not live in the project.
   Of the following, the MOST appropriate action for the housing assistant to take is to
   A. detain the boy and summon the police
   B. order the boy off the project grounds, warning him that he will be severely punished if caught on the grounds again
   C. take the knife away and report the name and address of the boy to the management office
   D. tell the boy that he was ruining a perfectly useful bench and warn him not to repeat this misdeed
   E. try to determine he reason for the boy's action in order to divert his interest to more desirable forms of play

   2.____

3. A tenant who recently won a television set tells you that there is interference in reception due to the intermittent operation of the oil burners in the boiler room beneath her apartment. She asks you to try to have this interference eliminated.
   Of the following, the MOST practical suggestion for you to make is to
   A. advise the tenant that she will have to remove the television set because it consumes an excessive amount of current
   B. inform the tenant that the television set is probably defective
   C. suggest that she have the television maintenance man install shielding devices on the oil burners

   3.____

2 (#1)

D. suggest that the tenant write to the Division of Management for advice on the matter
E. tell the tenant that you will discuss the problem with the building superintendent

4. A maintenance man has noticed that a number of new tenants have been throwing paper and other waste material out of the windows.
Of the following, the MOST practical way of reducing the incidence of violation of this tenancy rule by these tenants is to
   A. call a general meeting of tenants to discuss the need for compliance with the rules of tenancy
   B. inform these tenants by letter or visit of the rules of tenancy
   C. keep the new tenants under close observation until they have adjusted themselves
   D. post appropriate signs in conspicuous places
   E. warn these tenants that they may be subject to penalties if they persist in violating tenancy rules

4.____

5. Of the following, the MOST important item that should be noted by a housing assistant on his first visit to a newly occupied apartment is
   A. fingermarks on the newly painted woodwork
   B. leaking hot water tap
   C. nails hammered into the walls to hang pictures
   D. poor arrangement of furniture in the living room
   E. strong garbage odor in the kitchen

5.____

6. An attempt is being made at your housing project to stop children from marking the walls with chalk. Several tenants tell you that they saw the children of another tenant marking the walls.
Of the following, the MOST appropriate action to take in an attempt to remedy the situation is to
   A. concentrate your attention on these children to determine their guilt
   B. tell the tenants that nothing can be done unless the children are caught defacing the walls
   C. thank the tenants for their interest but take no action since factual evidence is lacking
   D. visit the home of the accused children to discuss the matter with their parents
   E. visit the home of the accused children to discuss with them the harmful nature of such actions and the availability of more desirable activities

6.____

7. You are informed that a tenant is providing temporary shelter in his apartment for an immigrant relative who plans to leave within a few months.
Of the following, the MOST advisable action to take first is to
   A. ascertain the availability of a larger apartment since they may conceivably stay longer
   B. ascertain the income and legal status of the relative
   C. inform the tenant that additional occupants are not permitted and that the relative must vacate as soon as possible

7.____

D. refer the tenant to a social agency providing assistance
E. attempt to find suitable quarters elsewhere for the relative

8. While making a special visit to a family, you notice that the apartment is in a dirty and unsanitary condition.
   Of the following, the MOST appropriate action to take is to
   A. discuss privately with the male head of the family the evident poor management of the household
   B. inform the tenant that such poor management is frowned upon and may be the basis for termination of tenancy
   C. make no reference to the condition but confine your attention to the purpose of your visit
   D. report the situation to the Housing Manager for possible referral to a private social agency
   E. suggest that the tenant take a course in homemaking at a nearby community center

9. A tenant tells you that her son has difficulty in finding playmates at a project playground because the other boys do not accept him into the games they play. She asks your help and advice.
   Of the following, the MOST advisable course of action for you to take is to
   A. ask the tenant to send a letter to the Management Office outlining the problem and its effect on her son
   B. refer the tenant to a child guidance clinic for remedial treatment of her son
   C. send the mother to the Building Superintendent who has charge of playground maintenance to have these cliques broken up
   D. suggest that the tenant accompany her son to the playground to urge the other boys to play with him
   E. suggest that the tenant have her son join one of the boys' clubs of the project

10. A porter employed at your project asks you if a friend of his whose application was processed by you has been approved as eligible for an apartment at your project.
    Of the following, the MOST appropriate action to take is to
    A. ascertain the relationship between the porter and the applicant before discussing his status
    B. discuss the facts of the situation confidentially with the porter to develop a cooperative relationship with him
    C. inform him of the tenant's status only if you actually know the final decision on this application
    D. inform the porter that the applicant will be notified shortly of the results of his application
    E. report to your superior that the porter has asked you to intercede on behalf of his friend

4 (#1)

11. The one of the following statements which was NOT characteristic of the Federal rent control law was that
    A. municipal governments may decontrol rents without the approval of the governor of the state
    B. state legislatures may decontrol rents with the approval of the governor of the state
    C. non-transient hotel apartments in the city are controlled
    D. so-called luxury apartments may be decontrolled under certain conditions
    E. rent controls were extended for a period of six months from the date of expiration of the previous law

11.____

12. Many laws affecting the welfare of the people have been considered by the present Congress for change, extension, or repeal.
    Of the following, the one which would probably affect tenants of public housing projects LEAST is the proposed
    A. change in Federal income tax laws
    B. extension of Old Age and Survivors Insurance
    C. repeal of margarine taxes
    D. revision of immigration quotas
    E. revision of minimum hourly wages

12.____

13. The feature of the low-rent housing program presented by a governor from a large state which distinguishes it from others in the field is its provision for
    A. decentralized mortgage control to insure greater responsiveness to local needs
    B. fair net operating income for builders of low-cost dwelling units
    C. low-interest loans by the state to private builders of low-cost dwelling units
    D. tax abatements to urban development companies
    E. supervision by the state of construction undertaken by limited dividend housing corporations

13.____

14. Under the current Federal rent control regulations, the one of the following which CANNOT be used as a basis for seeking to evict a tenant is the fact that the
    A. landlord wishes to have a member of his immediate family occupy the premises
    B. landlord himself wishes to occupy the premises
    C. property has been acquired by the city for the purpose of making a public improvement
    D. property has been taken over by a bank as a result of foreclosure proceedings
    E. landlord wishes to demolish the premises

14.____

15. The one of the following countries which is NOT a party to the North Atlantic Pact is
    A. Belgium   B. Iceland   C. Luxemburg
    D. Portugal   E. Sweden

15.____

16. The housing assistant is a *tyro* if he is MOST NEARLY a
    A. charlatan　　　B. martinent　　　C. novice
    D. scholar　　　E. talebearer

17. A tenant who is *adamant* in his complaints about the noise emanating from the neighboring apartment is MOST NEARLY
    A. belligerent　　　B. justified　　　C. petty
    D. spiteful　　　E. unyielding

18. The housing assistant, according to his supervisor's report, had performed his tasks *assiduously*.
    The word *assiduously* means MOST NEARLY
    A. diligently　　　B. expertly　　　C. inefficiently
    D. reluctantly　　　E. satisfactorily

19. The current *exigency* of affairs at the Authority was given as the reason for the decision.
    The word *exigency* means MOST NEARLY
    A. conduct　　　B. investigation　　　C. trend
    D. uncertainty　　　E. urgency

20. The discovery of the *defalcation* was made by the manager.
    The word *defalcation* means MOST NEARLY
    A. damage　　　B. error　　　C. fraud
    D. hoax　　　E. theft

21. The *halcyon* days that followed could not have been predicted.
    The word *halcyon* means MOST NEARLY
    A. ecstatic　　　B. eventful　　　C. festive
    D. frenzied　　　E. untroubled

22. The housing assistant submitted a *sententious* report after he had made his investigation.
    The word *sententious* means MOST NEARLY
    A. laudatory　　　B. pithy　　　C. tentative
    D. unfavorable　　　E. verbal

23. A housing assistant should be characterized as *saturnine* if he is MOST NEARLY
    A. apathetic　　　B. enigmatic　　　C. gloomy
    D. sarcastic　　　E. unreliable

24. A situation arising at a project is *anomalous* if the situation is MOST NEARLY
    A. dangerous　　　B. irritating　　　C. perplexing
    D. recurrent　　　E. unusual

25. The Housing Authority did what it could to *palliate* the condition about which the tenants had complained.
The word *palliate* means MOST NEARLY
   A. reconsider
   B. rectify
   C. relieve
   D. remedy
   E. remove

25.____

26. It has been claimed that subsidized housing for workers who cannot pay rent high enough to secure good housing on a profit basis is, in effect, subsidizing low wages for the benefit of parsimonious employers.
The defect of this argument is that
   A. it fails to distinguish between money wages and real wages
   B. sanitary and decent housing costs more than slums
   C. wage and hour legislation would then be unnecessary
   D. wages have not been high enough in the past, prior to the time subsidized housing became available, to enable the average worker to secure good housing
   E. wages would tend to remain at levels in existence at the time that subsidized housing becomes generally available to low-income families

26.____

27. The enforcement of existing or procurable legislation regarding public health, safety, and morals would eliminate slums without the use of public funds.
The defect of this argument is that
   A. compulsory increases in standards means higher rentals
   B. existing acceptable housing is still insufficient to meet housing needs
   C. it assumes the continuation of a high level of home building activity by private enterprise
   D. legislation regarding public welfare is absolutely necessary for civilized urban life
   E. proper exercise of the police power of the state can promote the public welfare

27.____

28. Human society in a slum area is extremely mixed. A majority of the adults are self-respecting, law-abiding working men and women in low-paid or irregular occupations who want to bring their children up right and have them get on in the world. A smaller group has been pushed down from a higher income level by illness, accident, or incompetence.
On the basis of the above statement, it would be MOST accurate to state that
   A. adults earning good salaries should not live in slum areas
   B. children who are raised in a slum are more likely to present problems of juvenile delinquency
   C. residents of slum areas include adults who formerly had a higher income level
   D. self-respecting, law-abiding working men and women in low-paid occupations are as likely to be found in slum areas as anywhere else
   E. tenants in substandard housing are sometimes prevented, by conditions they cannot control, from raising their children in the manner they would like

28.____

29. A considerable body of substandard housing can be made acceptable by repairs and modernization. For this reason and others, the volume of substandard housing is much greater than the volume reasonably recommended for demolition. On the other hand, any slum clearance scheme will involve the demolition of some houses which, if located elsewhere, would not need to be demolished. No locality large enough for neighborhood development is made up 100% of housing unfit for use.
On the basis of the above statement, it would be MOST correct to say that
    A. a combination of insanitary conditions exists only in slum areas which need to be redeveloped
    B. clearing slums always involves demolition of some acceptable housing
    C. localities which need to be redeveloped contain substandard housing only
    D. repairs and modernization are an acceptable substitute for redevelopment of a slum area
    E. the volume of substandard housing must of necessity increase as the age of existing housing increases

29._____

30. Zoning ordinances have generally served a highly useful purpose in preserving neighborhoods unspoiled for the greatest good of the greatest number. Zoning has been a boon to families of moderate means. The wealthy could always protect themselves by living in restricted districts or owning large estates. Working men well enough off to live in new sections have been helped too, those in older sections very little, those in slums not at all.
On the basis of this statement, it may be PROPERLY assumed that
    A. adequate zoning laws will, over a long period, rehabilitate slum areas
    B. business districts do not benefit from zoning laws
    C. home owners need the protection afforded by zoning laws
    D. new homes for families of moderate income can change the character of a decadent area
    E. zoning laws prevent the creation of slums

30._____

31. Complete absence of policy hampered the war housing program from the start. Operations were again centralized in the Federal government. As further appropriations were authorized, a dozen uncoordinated federal agencies began to scramble for a share of the purse. They competed for sites and personnel sometimes outbid one another. In one city, one agency actually blocked off another's streets.
On the basis of this statement, it would be MOST correct to assume that
    A. appropriations for war housing reflected wartime rush and confusion
    B. centralization of Federal war housing operations would have resulted in a more coordinated program
    C. centralized authority can bring order out of chaos
    D. overlapping functions and operations of different bureaus lead to inefficiency
    E. some of the mistakes made in emergency housing during World War II were repeated

31._____

32. It is highly important that in any approach to the reduction of the cost of building houses, careful attention should be given to the problems of depreciation and maintenance since savings in the original cost of building a house can easily be offset by heavy maintenance and repair bills if shoddy materials and workmanship are employed.
   On the basis of this statement, the LEAST accurat4e of the following statements is:
   A. Depreciation charges are always a factor to be considered in the true cost of houses.
   B. Good workmanship in building a house helps prevent physical deterioration.
   C. Heavy maintenance charges can easily offset part of the cost of building a house.
   D. Reduction in tax rates is not the only factor which contributes to a reduction in the true cost of houses.
   E. The original cost of building a house may not reflect its true cost.

32.____

33. Tearing down slums may be esthetically satisfying and emotionally soothing but it does not, of itself, improve the housing conditions of low-income families. Slum clearance tends to impose additional hardships on tenants and does nothing to remedy the underlying conditions.
    On the basis of the above statement, it would be MOST correct to state that
    A. healthful decent housing for low-income families implies the demolition of slums
    B. healthful decent housing within the means of low-income families must be provided before slums can be torn down
    C. low-income families are forced to live in slum areas
    D. slum clearance is a necessary preliminary to improving housing conditions of low-income families
    E. society must hold itself responsible for removing the causes of slums

33.____

Questions 34-42.

DIRECTIONS: Each of the items numbered 34 through 42 contains five underlined words, one of which is not in keeping with the meaning which the selection is evidently intended to carry. The five underlined words in each selection are reprinted after the selection. Indicate the letter in front of the one of the five words which does MOST to spoil the true meaning of the selection.

34. Urban expansion is basically an economic process, involving the mobility of business and manufacture, and trends in land values. As the central business district of a growing city expands, spilling out into the manufacturing area about it, the proximity of business and manufacturing with its noise, smoke, and traffic, make the area a less desirable one in which to live.
    A. mobility   B. trends   C. growing
    D. manufacturing   E. proximity

34.____

35. Inherent in the <u>processes</u> of urban growth, and the physical and social pattern it <u>produces</u>, is the breakdown of <u>community</u> life in the transitional areas of the city – the <u>socialization</u> of institutional forms and controls, the individuation of behavior and the <u>inability</u> of the local area to meet its own problems.
    A. processes
    B. produces
    C. community
    D. socialization
    E. inability

36. A blighted district is an area which has deteriorated from an <u>economic</u> standpoint and has therefore become less profitable to the city, the <u>public</u>, and the owner of its real estate. A <u>majority</u> of the buildings are old, and <u>fundamental</u> repairs are no longer made. It is a decaying area in which the cost of city services is <u>diminished</u>.
    A. economic
    B. public
    C. majority
    D. fundamental
    E. diminished

37. It would be <u>correct</u> to assume that <u>all</u> properly operated and conducted areas of a city show a <u>balance</u> between taxes paid by the area and <u>services</u> received from the city, and that those *in the red* are <u>necessarily</u> parasitic.
    A. correct
    B. all
    C. balance
    D. services
    E. necessarily

38. It is my belief that <u>planning</u> in the field of housing will be, at best, barren of results, and, at worst, exceedingly dangerous unless it is geared to the <u>market</u> for <u>new</u> homes expressed in terms of the <u>desires</u> of the families to be <u>rehoused</u>.
    A. planning
    B. market
    C. new
    D. desires
    E. rehoused

39. The result is that there are three governments with the power to clear slums, three governments <u>authorized</u> to engage in public housing activities. But for the sake of efficiency, <u>some</u> of the administration and construction should be performed by a single agency. It is logical that that agency should be the <u>local</u> housing authority.
    A. power
    B. authorized
    C. some
    D. construction
    E. local

40. The scope of city planning must be enlarged to include municipal acquisition of lands for development. Land not fitting into the pattern of <u>logical</u> development would be withdrawn from <u>zoning</u>. There should be <u>state</u> legislation permitting acquisition of vacant land <u>beyond</u> the city's borders and allowing cities to <u>prohibit</u> subdivisions which are economically disruptive.
    A. logical
    B. zoning
    C. state
    D. beyond
    E. prohibit

41. One of the principal <u>disadvantages</u> of setting <u>specific</u> limitations on the cost of public housing is the <u>flexibility</u> allowed localities with <u>varying</u> cost <u>differentials</u>.
    A. disadvantages
    B. specific
    C. flexibility
    D. varying
    E. differentials

10 (#1)

42. Probably the most effective way to eliminate <u>restrictive</u> practices in the building industry is to <u>develop</u> new materials and methods and improved building organizations which will substantially increase <u>efficiency</u> throughout the <u>consumption</u> and <u>distribution</u> process and thereby substantially reduce costs.
    A. restrictive
    B. develop
    C. efficiency
    D. consumption
    E. distribution

42._____

43. A project tenant who owns and drives a taxicab for a living reports, for a three-month period, an income of $2,500 after operating expenses of $250 have been considered. In addition, his tips are valued at 12% of his income before operating expenses.
    An estimate of his yearly income is MOST NEARLY
    A. $8,800
    B. $9,200
    C. $11,200
    D. $11,400
    E. $11,600

43._____

44. The maximum annual subsidy which can be paid by the State toward the operation of any low-rent housing project is the sum of the annual interest on the total original loan for building the project and 1% of the portion of the loan actually spent.
    If the original loan for a project was $8,000,000 at 1¾% interest, but only $7,500,000 was actually spent, then the MAXIMUM annual subsidy is
    A. $140,000
    B. $145,000
    C. $215,000
    D. $220,000
    E. $271,250

44._____

45. In 2016, the cost of repairs and maintenance at a certain housing project was $5,589 more than in 2015, representing an increase of 4.6%. A further increase at the same rate is anticipated for 2017.
    The cost of repairs and maintenance in 2017 will be MOST NEARLY
    A. $127,100
    B. $132,700
    C. $132,900
    D. $133,000
    E. an amount which cannot be determined from the given data

45._____

46. Each day a delivery truck used by the Housing Authority travels 25 miles from a project to a storehouse and 25 miles on the return trip. It travels at the rate of 30 miles per hour going to the storehouse and at the rate of 20 miles per hour returning.
    The average rate, in miles per hour, for the roundtrip is MOST NEARLY
    A. 24
    B. 25
    C. 26
    D. the square root of 600
    E. an amount which cannot be determined from the given data

46._____

11 (#1)

47. A report on the first 6,000 applications for apartments in a certain project containing 1,400 apartments indicated that those who were ineligible fell into four categories: 2,800 ineligible for reason A, 600 ineligible for reason B, 1,200 ineligible for reason C, and 400 ineligible for reason D.
If the same proportions continue for the remaining 21,500 applications, then the percentage of eligible applicants who can be given apartments in the project is MOST NEARLY
   A. 25   B. 30   C. 33   D. 40   E. 60

47.____

48. The number of applications for apartments in low-rent housing projects was 40,000 in 2014. The number of applications increased 5% in 2015, and increased again in 2016 by 6% over the 2015 total.
The percentage by which the 2016 figures exceed the 2014 figures is
   A. 5.3   B. 6.0   C. 11.0   D. 11.3   E. 30.0

48.____

49. The number of non-farm dwelling units constructed or pending construction in this country in the post-war period which were publicly financed is
   A. greater than the number which were privately financed
   B. approximately the same as the number which were privately financed
   C. less than the number which were privately financed
   D. greater than the number which were privately financed and required a smaller total expenditure
   E. approximately the same as the number which were privately financed and required a smaller total expenditure

49.____

50. It is generally agreed by those who have closely studied the housing shortage in this country that, of the new housing needed in the next decade to meet the shortage and to raise standards, the GREATEST part will be required to
   A. house families now seeking separate dwellings
   B. house new families formed during the period
   C. maintain a suitable percentage of vacancies
   D. replace dwellings dropping out of the market
   E. replace substandard dwelling units

50.____

KEY (CORRECT ANSWERS)

1. A	11. A	21. E	31. D	41. C
2. D	12. D	22. B	32. C	42. D
3. E	13. C	23. C	33. B	43. D
4. B	14. D	24. E	34. D	44. C
5. B	15. E	25. C	35. D	45. C
6. D	16. C	26. D	36. E	46. A
7. C	17. E	27. B	37. A	47. B
8. B	18. A	28. C	38. D	48. D
9. E	19. E	29. B	39. C	49. C
10. D	20. E	30. C	40. B	50. E

TEST 2

DIRECTIONS: Each question or incomplete statement is followed by several suggested answers or completions. Select the one that BEST answers the question or completes the statement. *PRINT THE LETTER OF THE CORRECT ANSWER IN THE SPACE AT THE RIGHT.*

Questions 1-4.

DIRECTIONS: Questions 1 through 4 are to be answered SOLELY on the basis of the data given in the following table.

ESTIMATED DISTRIBUTION OF NON-FARM FAMILIES, BY INCOME CLASSES
(Number of Families in Thousands)

Net Money Income Class	Families of 2 or More Persons		Families of 1 Person		Total Families	
	Number	Percent	Number	Percent	Number	Percent
Under $10,000	2,626	8.0	1,062	26.7	3,688	10.0
$10,000-14,990	4,595	14.0	930	23.4	5,525	15.0
$15,000-19,990	5,251	16.0	744	18.7	5,995	16.0
$20,000-24,990	5,251	16.0	513	12.9	5,764	16.0
$25,000-34,990	8,861	27.0	413	10.4	9,274	25.0
$35,000-54,990	4,266	13.0	215	5.4	4,481	12.0
$55,000 and over	1,969	6.0	99	2.5	2,068	6.0
TOTAL	32,819	100.0	3,976	100.0	36,795	100.0

1. The number of income categories in which the percentage of one-person families exceeds that of two-or-more person families is
   A. none   B. 1   C. 2   D. 3   E. 4

   1.____

2. The number of non-farm families which earn under $35,000 is MOST NEARLY
   A. 27 thousand   B. 30 thousand   C. 30 million
   D. 35 million   E. 82%

   2.____

3. The number of income categories in which one-person families form the higher proportion of families is
   A. none   B. 1   C. 2   D. 3   E. 4

   3.____

4. The percentage of all families earning more than $25,000 which is represented by families of two or more persons is MOST NEARLY
   A. 18.3   B. 43   C. 46   D. 89   E. 95

   4.____

Questions 5-8.

DIRECTIONS: Column I lists four items, numbered 5 through 8, each of which is to be matched with one of the choices given in Column II. For each item of Column I, write in the space at the right of the question the letter in front of the acceptable choice in Column II.

Column I

5. Supervises Federal savings and loan associations

6. Insures qualified lending institutions against loss on loans made for the construction of low-cost homes

7. Administration of projects built under the U.S. Housing Act

8. Responsible for the disposition of Federally-owned war housing

Column II

A. Federal Housing Administration
B. State Housing Administration
C. Home Loan Bank Board
D. National Housing Council
E. Public Housing Administration

5.____

6.____

7.____

8.____

9. The author of THE SEVEN MYTHS OF HOUSING is
   A. Catherine Bauer
   B. Raymond M. Foley
   C. Philip M. Klutznick
   D. Lewis Mumford
   E. Nathan Straus

9.____

10. The author of HOUSING THE MASSES is
    A. Charles Abrams
    B. Carol Aronovici
    C. Langdon W. Post
    D. Mary M. Simkhovitch
    E. Robert F. Wagner

10.____

Questions 11-13.

DIRECTIONS: Column I lists three items, numbered 11 through 13, which list the titles and authors of three publications, each of which is to be matched with one of the subjects given in Column II. For each item of Column I, write in the space to the right of the question the letter in front of the subject in Column II which BEST expresses the central theme or major area presented in each publication.

Column I | Column II

11. INTRODUCTION TO HOUSING by Edith Wood
12. GREENBELT COMMUNITIES
13. A MILLION HOMES A YEAR by Dorothy Rosenman

A. Broad aspects of housing, construction costs, and community planning
B. Economic and social effects of poor housing; how areas become slums
C. Explanation of the public housing program from the tenant's standpoint
D. Study of Black life in several selected Southern cities before and after public housing
E. First completely planned communities built in the U.S.
F. Interracial planning for community organization
G. Post-war housing shortage in the U.S.

11. ____
12. ____
13. ____

14. The right of public agencies to use the power of eminent domain for slum clearance and public housing indicates that these activities are presently considered
    A. a socio-economic advantage
    B. necessary to legalize housing subsidies
    C. to be for private use with public control
    D. to be for public health purposes
    E. to be for public purpose and use

14. ____

15. The right of a state to take measures to protect the health and welfare of its citizens is MOST NEARLY a definition of
    A. a general welfare clause
    B. police power
    C. public responsibility
    D. sanitary code
    E. sovereign power

15. ____

16. A system under which project rents are based on income and size of family instead of being based exclusively on the number of rooms in the apartment is known as _____ rent.
    A. economic
    B. graded
    C. subsidized
    D. surcharge
    E. welfare

16. ____

17. One of the features of the Taft-Ellender-Wagner Housing Bill was its desire to attract more private capital to the housing field by guaranteeing a minimum return on the investment while limiting the maximum return.
    This provision is known as
    A. loan guarantee
    B. mortgage insurance
    C. redevelopment subsidy
    D. Title VI housing
    E. yield insurance

17. ____

4 (#2)

18. The one of the following items which is NOT generally included in the capital cost of housing construction is
    A. amortization of mortgage
    B. contractor's profit
    C. cost of labor
    D. cost of land
    E. cost of materials

    18.____

19. Local constructions which are required as one condition for the granting of federal subsidies for low-rent housing projects CANNOT be in the form of
    A. cash
    B. grants
    C. loan guarantees
    D. tax exemptions
    E. tax remission

    19.____

20. The CHIEF purpose of housing constructed under the Lanham Act was to
    A. alleviate unemployment
    B. house employees in defense and war industries
    C. house transient migratory workers
    D. permit the demolition of slums
    E. provide a yardstick for estimating development and operating costs of future low-rent housing

    20.____

21. The permanent consolidation under one agency of all Federal activities relating to housing was accomplished by the
    A. Federal Housing Policy Act
    B. Government Corporations Act of 1948
    C. Reorganization Plan of 1947
    D. Taft-Ellender-Wagner Act
    E. none of the above

    21.____

22. Public housing is for low-income families who cannot afford to pay enough to cause private enterprise in their locality or metropolitan area to build an adequate supply of decent, safe, and sanitary dwellings for their use.
    The above formal statement of policy concerning who needs public housing was made by the
    A. Federal Public Housing Authority officials
    B. National Association of Housing officials
    C. National Housing Council
    D. United States Housing Act
    E. President of the United States to guide project activities of the Public Works Administration

    22.____

23. The ratio of annual income to rental which applies to a veteran with one child living in a state-financed low-rent project for continued occupancy is
    A. 5 to 1   B. 6 to 1   C. 7 to 1   D. 8 to 1   E. no set ratio

    23.____

24. The MAXIMUM percentage of the cost of developing and building a low-rent housing project which may be advanced as a loan by the state is _____ the percentage which may be advanced by
    A. greater than; the Federal government
    B. the same as; the Federal government
    C. less than; the Federal government
    D. greater than; the Federal government if the project is for veterans only
    E. greater than; a city government

25. It is the present policy of the management of state-aided public housing projects to grant FIRST preference to eligible applicants who are families
    A. of veterans
    B. displaced from the site upon which the project was built
    C. of low income who are unable to find suitable housing
    D. of veterans in emergency temporary projects
    E. of veterans in substandard housing

26. The one of the following statements which is NOT characteristic of a housing company organized under the State Public Housing Law is:
    A. The Commissioner of Housing must approve building plans before construction is begun.
    B. The consent of the Commissioner of Housing must be obtained before it is permitted to incorporate.
    C. The land necessary for one of its projects must be acquired by negotiation with property owners of the area
    D. The rents to be charged the tenants are controlled by law.
    E. The stockholders may receive only a limited annual dividend.

27. Of the following, the statement about legal restrictions on housing in the city that is NOT correct is:
    A. According to the Multiple Dwelling Law, multiple dwellings of frame construction may not be erected at the present time.
    B. The Multiple Dwelling Law applies to all kinds and classes of multiple dwellings including those erected prior to passage of the law.
    C. The Multiple Dwelling Law has provisions for minimum floor areas for rooms of apartments.
    D. The Tenement House Law of 1901 outlawed existing old law tenements.
    E. The Zoning Resolution regulates the specific use of buildings erected after the passage of the resolution and not those previously erected.

28. The basis upon which taxes are paid by the City Housing Authority for projects built by funds from a state loan is
    A. a fixed percentage, set by law, of the rental income of the project
    B. the variable amount, depending on the local tax rate
    C. the amount of tax arrears upon the site and the buildings on it prior to the construction of the project
    D. the value of the site and the project buildings
    E. the valuation of the site and the buildings on it prior to the construction of the project

29. The right of a housing authority to acquire property in excess of that needed for a project is granted by state law MAINLY because
    A. a considerable surrounding area is necessary for placing the materials and equipment required during construction
    B. it is not generally possible to determine exactly the amount of property needed for a project
    C. it may occasionally be necessary to shift the site of the project slightly during construction
    D. the area surrounding the project should be protected from undesirable characteristics
    E. the total area required by a project should exceed the area actually occupied by the project buildings

30. Assume that an applicant for an apartment in a public housing project objects to answering a question concerning whether he has any income other than which he receives from his regular employment.
    The BEST course of action for the housing assistant to take is to
    A. advise the applicant that he is ineligible and terminate the interview
    B. advise the applicant to reconsider his refusal to answer and then ask the question again
    C. go on to the next question and return to this one later in the interview when better rapport has been established
    D. inform the applicant of the reason for asking the question and tell him he must answer
    E. tell the applicant that the question is required by law and that he must answer

31. The provision in a public housing project of social and community facilities over and above adequate shelter is
    A. *desirable*, because it provides coordination of adult activities
    B. *desirable*, since such facilities are an essential part of a healthy social environment
    C. *desirable*, since such facilities may not be available otherwise
    D. *undesirable*, because it promotes a paternalistic attitude on the part of management
    E. *undesirable*, because it unduly increases overall operating costs

32. More damage has been done to the health of children of the United States by a sense of chronic inferiority due to consciousness of life in substandard dwellings than by all the defective plumbing whose dwellings may contain.
    Of the following, the MOST reasonable conclusion that may be drawn from this statement is that
    A. esthetic satisfaction in the home and its surroundings has some bearing on the physical well-being of children
    B. normal physical and mental development is not possible when children are conscious of the substandard nature of their homes
    C. psychiatric treatment is a necessary component of the adjustment of the children of slum families after transfer to public housing projects

D. the physical aspects of good housing are far less important in the healthful development of children than the provision of adequate play facilities
E. the replacement of defective plumbing can have little effect on the health of children in slum areas

33. Upon the request of a tenant, a stoppage in a toilet fixture caused by a dropped hairbrush was removed. This was the third instance in six months of such service for this tenant.
Current practice in the management of large projects suggests that
    A. a charge be made for this service repeatedly required by a tenant
    B. a charge be made only if the tenant is known to be unusually neglectful and irresponsible
    C. no charge be made, but the tenant be warned that the need for such service is evidence of willful neglect
    D. no charge for such special service be made since tenants are selected on the basis of low income
    E. tenants be taught how to make minor repairs to plumbing fixtures to avoid excessive service requests

33.____

34. Slum areas and bad housing are expensive to a city CHIEFLY because
    A. crime and delinquency flourish there
    B. higher rents are usually charged there than the tenants can afford
    C. more city service of all kinds need to be provided
    D. such areas generally represent the larger portion of the city
    E. the tuberculosis death rate is many times higher than in other areas

34.____

35. Of the following, the MOST important problem in the assembly of land for urban redevelopment of slum areas by private companies is the
    A. excessive cost of demolition
    B. high cost of land
    C. inadequacy of municipal services in slum areas
    D. rate of obsolescence in slum areas
    E. unattractiveness of slum areas

35.____

36. Of the following, the GREATEST difficulty in connection with a cooperative housing project is usually
    A. obtaining the purchasers of apartments
    B. purchasing the land
    C. dealing with the building contractors
    D. allocating apartments so all are satisfied
    E. operating the project

36.____

37. When a housing assistant visits the home of an applicant to obtain necessary eligibility verification, she finds present in the room an eight-year-old son.
In order to conduct the interview properly, the MOST reasonable action that the housing assistant should take with respect to the boy is to
    A. allow the boy to stay but warn him not to make any comment during the interview
    B. ask the parent to send the child to another room to emphasize the confidential nature of the visit
    C. elicit from the child details of his interests, school record, and health and demonstrate to the parent the attitude of management
    D. greet the child, but direct the interview toward the parent or adult members of the family
    E. ignore the child completely to avoid embarrassing him

38. When interviewing an applicant who is visiting the management office for the first time, the MOST desirable way to start the interview is to
    A. ask the applicant to supply proof of identity and present address before beginning the interview
    B. ask the applicant objective questions concerning his difficulty in securing adequate housing
    C. explain the purpose of the interview before reviewing his application with him
    D. place the applicant at ease by allowing him to talk freely about his need for housing
    E. tell the applicant that all statements he will make will be subject to investigation and verification

39. The PRINCIPAL purpose of the Police Athletic League is the
    A. administration of recreational and social activities for the members of the Police Department
    B. coordination of athletic activities in parks and playgrounds not under the control of the Department of Parks
    C. provision of recreational activities as part of preventive follow-up for former adult offenders
    D. provision of recreation and social services for children in slum areas
    E. supervisory control of social clubs and private youth organizations

40. A family appeals to you for assistance when the wage earner loses his job in private industry. They inform you that there are no reserves or resources to tide the family over the uncertain period of unemployment.
The MOST appropriate referrals that should be made are to the
    A. Division of Unemployment Insurance and a private social agency
    B. Division of Unemployment Insurance and the Department of Social Services
    C. State Division of Workmen's Compensation and the Department of Social Services
    D. Department of Social Services and the State Division of Workmen's Compensation
    E. Household Finance Corporation and the Department of Social Services

KEY (CORRECT ANSWERS)

1.	D	11.	B	21.	C	31.	B
2.	C	12.	E	22.	D	32.	A
3.	A	13.	A	23.	C	33.	A
4.	E	14.	E	24.	A	34.	C
5.	C	15.	B	25.	B	35.	B
6.	A	16.	B	26.	C	36.	A
7.	E	17.	E	27.	D	37.	D
8.	E	18.	A	28.	E	38.	C
9.	E	19.	C	29.	D	39.	D
10.	B	20.	B	30.	D	40.	B

EXAMINATION SECTION

TEST 1

DIRECTIONS: Each question or incomplete statement is followed by several suggested answers or completions. Select the one that BEST answers the question or completes the statement. *PRINT THE LETTER OF THE CORRECT ANSWER IN THE SPACE AT THE RIGHT.*

1. Assume that a supervisor finds that his employees have become fatigued from doing a very long and repetitious job.
   The one of the following which would be the BEST way to relieve this fatigue is to
   A. assign other work so that the employees can switch to different assignments in the middle of the day
   B. let the employees listen to a radio while they work
   C. break the job down into very small parts so that each employee can concentrate on one simple task
   D. allow the employees to take frequent rest periods

   1._____

2. Assume that one of your subordinates is injured and will be out for at least six weeks.
   Of the following, the BEST way to handle the work normally assigned to this person is to
   A. allow the work to remain uncompleted until the injured person returns, since he is the one who can BEST do this work
   B. divide this work equally among the persons under your supervision who can do this work
   C. do all the work yourself
   D. give the injured person's work to the most efficient member of your staff

   2._____

3. Suppose that another supervisor tells you about a new way to organize some of your unit's work. The idea sounds good to you. However, before you were in this unit, a similar plan was tried and it failed.
   The MOST important thing for you to do FIRST is to
   A. find out why the previous attempt failed
   B. suggest that the other supervisor tell his idea to top management
   C. try the plan to see whether it works
   D. find proof that the plan has worked elsewhere

   3._____

4. One of your subordinates comes to you with a grievance. You discuss it with him so that you may fully understand the problem as he sees it.
   However, since you are uncertain as to the proper answer, you should
   A. tell him that you cannot help him with this problem
   B. tell him that you will have to check further and make an appointment to see him again
   C. send him to see your immediate superior for a solution to the problem
   D. ask him to find out from his co-workers whether this problem has come up before

   4._____

5. A supervisor reprimanded one of his subordinates severely for making a serious error in judgment while performing an assignment for which he had volunteered.
The supervisor's action was
   A. *incorrect*, chiefly because in the future the worker will probably try to avoid taking on responsibility
   B. *correct*, chiefly because this will insure that the worker will not make the same mistake in the future
   C. *correct*, chiefly because the worker should be discouraged from using his own judgment on the job
   D. *incorrect*, chiefly because the reprimand came too late to correct the error that had already been made

6. Of the following, the BEST way for a supervisor to inform all his subordinates of a change in lunch rules is, in MOST cases, to
   A. call a staff meeting
   B. tell each one individually
   C. issue a memorandum
   D. tell one or two employees to pass the word around

7. For a supervisor to assign work giving only general instructions to his subordinate would be advisable when
   A. the supervisor is confident that the worker knows how to do the job
   B. the assignment is a simple one
   C. the subordinate is himself a supervisory employee
   D. errors in the work will not cause serious delay

8. One of the DISADVANTAGES of setting minimum standards of performance for custodial employees is that
   A. such standards eliminate the basis for evaluating employees
   B. the custodial employees may keep their performance at the minimum level
   C. standards are always subject to change
   D. the supervisor may feel that his initiative is being restricted

9. One of your subordinates has been functioning below his usual level. You feel that something of a personal nature may be affecting his work. When you ask him casually whether anything is wrong, he says everything is fine.
As a next step, it would be BEST to
   A. make frequent casual and humorous comments about the poor quality of his work but refrain, at this time, from any serious discussion
   B. warn him that failure to maintain his customary level of performance might result in disciplinary action
   C. express your concern privately and reveal your interest in the reason for his change in work performance
   D. discuss with him the work of another employee, suggesting that the other employee would be a good example to follow

10. Assume you are teaching a new job to one of your subordinates. After you have demonstrated the job, you can BEST maintain the worker's interest by
    A. showing him training films about the job
    B. giving him printed material that explains why the job is important
    C. having him observe other workers do the job
    D. letting him attempt to do the job by himself under supervision

11. *Insubordination is sometimes a protest against inferior or arbitrary leadership.*
    For the supervisor, the MOST basic implication of the above statement is:
    A. Accusations of insubordination are easy to make, but usually difficult to prove.
    B. Insubordination cannot be permitted if an organization wishes to remain effective.
    C. When an employee discusses an order instead of carrying it out, he has not understood it.
    D. When an employee questions an order, review it to make sure it is reasonable.

12. In appraising a subordinate's mistakes, a supervisor should ALWAYS consider the
    A. absolute number of mistakes, without regard to severity
    B. number of mistakes in proportion to the number of decisions made
    C. total number of mistakes made by other, regardless of assignment
    D. number of mistakes which were discovered upon higher review

13. If you are the supervisor of an office in which the work frequently involves lifting heavy boxes, you should instruct your staff in the proper method of lifting to avoid injury.
    In giving these instructions, you should stress that a person lifting heavy objects MUST
    A. keep his feet close together
    B. bend at the waist
    C. keep his back as straight as possible
    D. use his back muscles to straighten up

14. Of the following, the BEST qualified supervisor is one who
    A. knows the basic principles and procedures of all the jobs which he supervises
    B. has detailed working knowledge of all aspects of the job he supervises but knows little about principles of supervision
    C. is able to do exceptionally well at least one of the jobs which he supervises and as some knowledge of the others
    D. knows little or nothing about most of the jobs which he supervises but knows the principles of supervision

15. The rate at which an employee will learn will vary according to a number of considerations.
    Of the following, which is LEAST likely to be controllable by the supervisor or the trainer? The
    A. manner in which the material is presented
    B. state of readiness of the learner
    C. scheduling of practice sessions
    D. nature of the material

16. When considering whether to use written material rather than oral instructions as a means of giving instructions to employees, the one of the following which should be given GREATEST consideration is the employees'
    A. personal preferences
    B. attitude toward supervision
    C. general educational level
    D. salary level

17. Assume that one of your subordinates has been assigned to attend job training classes.
    The one of the following which would probably be the BEST evidence of the success of the course is that the employee
    A. feels that he has learned something
    B. continues to study after the course is over
    C. has had a good class record
    D. improves in his work performance

18. Of the following, the situation LEAST likely to result if a supervisor shows favoritism toward particular employees is
    A. laxity in the work of the favored employees
    B. resentment from the other, less-favored employees
    C. increased ability among the favored employees
    D. lowering of morale among employees

19. The one of the following reasons for evaluating employees' performance, whether done formally or informally, which is NOT considered to be POSITIVE in nature is to
    A. give individual counsel to employees
    B. motivate employees toward improvement
    C. provide recognition of superior service
    D. set penalties for substandard performance

20. Assume that, because there has been an unexpected and temporary increase in the short-term work of your unit, you have had temporarily assigned to you several staff members from another agency.
    Of the following, in dealing with these employees, it would be LEAST advisable to
    A. assign them to long-term projects
    B. organize tasks so that they can begin work immediately
    C. set standards, making allowances to give them time to learn your ways
    D. direct them in the same way, in general, as you do your regular staff

21. It has been suggested that one way to increase employee productivity would be to require employees dealing with the public to have proficiency in a relevant foreign language.
    Of the following, the MAJOR reason for implementing such a proposal, from the viewpoint of effective public administration, would be to
    A. encourage the foreign-born to learn English
    B. exchange information more rapidly and accurately
    C. increase the public prestige of the agency
    D. stimulate ethnic pride among all groups

22. Assume that the clerk who normally keeps your unit's records will be on vacation for four weeks.
    If other clerks are equally qualified to keep these records, your BEST choice to replace the clerk would be the person who
    A. has skills which are needed least for other duties during this period
    B. volunteers for this work
    C. is next in turn for a special assignment
    D. has handled this task before

23. Assume that you have under your supervision several young clerical employees who have the bad habit of fooling around when they should be working.
    Of the following, the BEST disciplinary action to take would be to
    A. ignore it; these young people will outgrow it
    B. join in the fun briefly in order to bring it to a quicker end each time it occurs
    C. bring to their attention the fact that this behavior is not acceptable and if it continues shift the make-up of the group to keep these young persons apart
    D. warn them that this type of behavior is reason for dismissal and be quick to make an example of the first one who starts it again

24. Seeking the advice of community leaders has human relations value for a public agency in planning or executing its programs CHIEFLY because it
    A. allows for the keeping of careful records concerning individual suggestions
    B. lets community leaders know that the agency has regard for their opinions
    C. permits the agency to state in writing which programs seem most appropriate
    D. unifies community leaders against the programs of competing private agencies

25. Good community relations is often action-oriented.
    Which of the following activities of a public agency is LEAST likely to be considered as action-oriented by the people of a local community?
    A. Conducting a survey to gather information about the local community
    B. Extending the use of a facility to those previously excluded
    C. Providing a service that was formerly non-existent
    D. Removing something considered objectionable by the local community

KEY (CORRECT ANSWERS)

1.	A	11.	D
2.	B	12.	B
3.	A	13.	C
4.	B	14.	A
5.	A	15.	B
6.	C	16.	C
7.	A	17.	D
8.	B	18.	D
9.	C	19.	D
10.	D	20.	A

21. B
22. A
23. C
24. B
25. A

TEST 2

DIRECTIONS: Each question or incomplete statement is followed by several suggested answers or completions. Select the one that BEST answers the question or completes the statement. *PRINT THE LETTER OF THE CORRECT ANSWER IN THE SPACE AT THE RIGHT.*

1. Methods of communication with employees are of three types: oral, written, and visual.
   A MAJOR advantage of the written word is that it
   A. insures that content will remain unchanged no matter how many persons may be involved in its transmission
   B. facilitates two-way communication in delicate or confidential situations
   C. strengthens chain-of-command procedures in transmission of information and instruction by requiring the use of prescribed channels
   D. encourages the active participation of employees in the solution of complicated problems

   1._____

2. The use of the conference technique in training often requires more preparatory work on the part of the trainer than does a good lecture PRIMARILY because
   A. a conference would cover material of a more technical nature
   B. the trainer will be required to supply more printed material to the participants
   C. a conference usually involves a greater number of trainees
   D. the trainer must be prepared for a wide variety of possible occurrences

   2._____

3. The one of the following which is NOT an advantage of the lecture over most other methods of training is that it can be given
   A. over the radio or on record   B. to large numbers of trainees
   C. without interruptions   D. with little preparation

   3._____

4. Of the following, the one which is LEAST appropriate as a purpose for using an employee attitude survey is to
   A. develop a supervisory training program
   B. learn the identity of dissatisfied employees
   C. re-evaluate employee relations policies
   D. re-orient publications designed for employees

   4._____

5. The competent trainer seeks to become knowledgeable both in the work of the agency and in the duties of the positions for which he is to conduct training. Of the following, the GREATEST practical value that result when the trainer gains such knowledge is that
   A. he will be more likely to instruct employees to perform their work in a manner consistent with actual practice
   B. all levels of staff will be favorably impressed by a display of interest in the agency and its work
   C. employees will become familiar with the trainer and will not consider him an outsider
   D. the trainer will gain an accurate picture of the capacity of each employee for training

   5._____

6. Assume that you, the supervisor of a small office, are involved in planning the reorganization of your bureau's work. Management has decided not to inform your staff of the reorganization until the plans are completed.
   If one of your subordinates tells you that he has heard a rumor about reorganization of the department, you should reply that
   A. the reorganization involves the bureau, not the department
   B. you haven't heard anything about departmental reorganization and that he should stop spreading rumors
   C. you will inform your staff at the appropriate time if any definite plans are made involving a reorganization
   D. you do not know what is being planned but will ask your superior for details

7. Of the following training methods, the one in which the trainee's role is usually LEAST active is the _____ method.
   A. case-study
   B. conference
   C. group discussion
   D. lecture

8. Differences in morale between two work groups can sometimes be attributed to differences in the supervision they receive.
   Of the following, the behavior MOST characteristic of a supervisor of a group with high morale is that he
   A. assigns the least difficult tasks to employees with the most seniority
   B. is concerned primarily with his ultimate responsibility, production
   C. delegates authority and responsibility to his staff
   D. is lenient with his workers when they violate rules

9. Informal performance evaluations of individual employees, prepared systematically and regularly over a period of several years, are considered to be useful to a supervisor PRIMARILY because
   A. he will be able to assign tasks based only on these records
   B. unlike formal records, since they are fitted to the characteristics of individual employees, they provide for quick comparisons
   C. he need not discuss them with employees, since they are informal
   D. whatever personnel action he recommends can be substantiated by cumulative records

10. When instructing first-line supervisors in the proper method of evaluating the performance of probationary employees, it is LEAST important for a higher-level supervisor to
    A. explain in detail the standards to be used
    B. inform them of the possibility of higher management review
    C. caution them concerning common errors of evaluation
    D. mention the purposes of probationary employee evaluation

11. Assume that your agency is considering abolishing its official performance rating system but that you, a supervisor of a fairly large office, would like to devise a system for your own use.
    The FIRST step in setting up a system would be to
    A. decide what factors and personal characteristics are important and should be rated
    B. compare several rating methods to see which would be easiest to use
    C. have a private conference with each employee to discuss his performance
    D. set specific standards of employee performance, allowing your workers to make suggestions

12. The basic organizational structure of a municipal agency may have come about for several reasons.
    Of the following, the MOST important influence on the nature of its structure is the agency's
    A. professional attitude
    B. public reputation
    C. overall goal
    D. staff morale

13. The term *formal organization* refers to that organization structure agreed upon by top management whereas the term *informal organization* refers to the more spontaneous and flexible organizational ties developed by subordinates.
    The one of the following which BEST describes the usual *informal organization* is that it represents a(n)
    A. destructive system of relationships which should be eliminated
    B. concealed system of relationships whose goals are the same as management's
    C. actual system of relationships which should be recognized
    D. dysfunctional system of relationships which should be ignored

14. The reluctance of supervisors to delegate work to subordinates when they should is GENERALLY due to the supervisor's
    A. feelings of insecurity in work situations
    B. need to acquire additional experience
    C. inability to exercise control over his subordinates
    D. lack of technical knowledge

15. Assume that you have just been made the supervisor of a group of people you did not know before.
    For you to talk casually with each of your new subordinates with the purpose of getting to know them personally would be
    A. *advisable*, chiefly because subordinates have more confidence in a supervisor who shows personal interest in them
    B. *inadvisable*, chiefly because subordinates resent having their supervisor ask about their outside interests
    C. *advisable*, chiefly because one of the supervisor's main concerns should be to help his subordinates with their personal problems
    D. *inadvisable*, chiefly because a supervisor should not allow his relations with his subordinates to be influenced by their personalities

16. It has been found that high-producing subdivisions of organizations usually have supervisors whose behavior is employee-centered, whereas low-producing units usually have supervisors whose behavior is work-centered.
    Therefore, it could be concluded from these findings that
    A. a high-producing unit may cause a supervisor to be authoritarian
    B. a low-producing unit may cause a supervisor to be work-centered
    C. close supervision usually increases production
    D. employee-centered leadership may reduce production

17. A recent study in managerial science showed that, as the amount of praise increased and amount of criticism decreased, the supervisor was more likely to be perceived by his subordinates as being
    A. concerned with their career advancement
    B. production oriented, through subtle intimidation
    C. seeking personal satisfaction, irrespective of production
    D. uncertain of the subordinates' reliability

18. The power to issue directives or instructions to employees is derived from employees as much as from management.
    It follows MOST logically from this statement that
    A. attitudes toward management can be changed
    B. emphasis on discipline is needed
    C. authority is dependent upon acceptance
    D. employees should be properly supervised for work to be done

19. "In the decision-making process, it is a rare problem that has only one possible solution. Such a solution should be suspected of being nothing but a plausible argument for a preconceived idea."
    The author of the foregoing quotation apparently does NOT believe that
    A. there is usually only one possible solution to a problem
    B. the risks involved in any solution should be weighed against expected gains
    C. each alternative should be evaluated to determine the effort needed
    D. actions should be based on the urgency of problems

20. The supervisor who relies on punitive discipline to enforce his authority is putting limits on the potential of his leadership. Fear of punishment may secure obedience, but it destroys initiative. Such a supervisor's autocratic methods have cut off upward communications.
    Of the following, the major DISADVANTAGE of such autocratic behavior is that
    A. difficulties in the supervision of his subordinates will arise if limits are placed on the supervisor's responsibility
    B. policies that affect the public will be changed too frequently
    C. the supervisor will apply punishment subjectively rather than objectively
    D. instructions will be obeyed to the letter, regardless of changing circumstances

21. The need for a supervisor to carefully coordinate and direct the work of his unit increases as the work becomes   21.____
    A. more routine
    B. more specialized
    C. less complex
    D. less technical

22. The MAIN goal of discipline as used by a supervisor should be to   22.____
    A. keep the employees' respect
    B. influence behavior, so that work will be completed properly
    C. encourage the employees to work faster
    D. set an example for others

23. One of your subordinates has exhibited discourtesy and non-cooperation on several occasions.   23.____
    Of the following, the MOST appropriate attitude for you to adopt in dealing with this problem is that
    A. disciplinary measures for such an individual generally creates additional problems
    B. failure to correct such behavior may lead to worse offenses
    C. it is a mistake to make an issue out of minor infractions
    D. the harsher the medicine, the faster the cure

24. Assume that an employee has complained to you, his supervisor, that he cannot concentrate on his work because two of his co-workers make too much noise. You pay particular attention to these employees for several days and do not find them making excessive noise.   24.____
    The NEXT step you should take in handling this grievance is to
    A. have a talk with all three employees, urging them to cooperate and be considerate of one another
    B. arrange for the complainant to change his work location to a place away from the two co-workers
    C. talk to the complainant to find out if the complaint he made to you is the real cause of his dissatisfaction
    D. tell the complainant that you have found his grievance to be unfounded

25. In planning the application of an existing agency program to a local community, it is generally necessary to discover relevant problems and possibilities for service.   25.____
    Of the following, the BEST way to learn about such problems and possibilities for service would usually be to
    A. begin the program on a full-scale basis and await reactions
    B. seek opinions and advice from community residents and leaders
    C. hold staff meetings with agency employees who have worked in similar communities
    D. study official federal reports about already completed programs of the same kind

KEY (CORRECT ANSWERS)

1.	A	11.	A
2.	D	12.	C
3.	D	13.	C
4.	B	14.	A
5.	A	15.	A
6.	C	16.	B
7.	D	17.	A
8.	C	18.	C
9.	D	19.	A
10.	B	20.	D

21. B
22. B
23. B
24. C
25. B

TEST 3

DIRECTIONS: Each question or incomplete statement is followed by several suggested answers or completions. Select the one that BEST answers the question or completes the statement. *PRINT THE LETTER OF THE CORRECT ANSWER IN THE SPACE AT THE RIGHT.*

1. Which of the following characteristics would be LEAST detrimental to a supervisor in his efforts to set up and maintain good relations with other supervisors with whom he must deal in the course of his duties?
    A. Not getting involved in consultation on any supervisory problems they might have
    B. Indicating that they should improve their supervising methods and offering suggestions on how to do so
    C. Emphasizing his own role as a member of management
    D. Sharing information which has proved useful in his unit

    1.____

2. Both trainers and supervisors might agree that there is usually a best way to do a particular job. Yet a supervisor or instructor sometimes does not teach a new employee the best way, the most efficient way, to do a complex job. Sometimes, in such cases, the supervisor temporarily changes the sequence of operations, increases the number of steps needed to do a job, or makes other changes in the method, which then deviates from the one considered most efficient.
   When is such a difference in approach MOST justified when teaching a new employee a complex job?
    A. When the changes in approach correspond to the learning ability of the new employee
    B. When the new employee's performance on the job is closely supervised to compensate for a change in approach
    C. Where the steps in performing the task have not been defined in a manual of procedures
    D. When the instructor has ideas of improving upon the methods for doing the job

    2.____

3. Considerable thought in the field of management is directed toward the advantages and disadvantages of authoritarian methods of influencing behavior, and, in the so-called authoritarian model, a nucleus of rather consistent ideas prevail.
   Which of the following is LEAST characteristic of an administrative system based on the authoritarian model?
    A. A conviction of a need for order and efficiency in a world consisting mainly of people who lack direction and incentive
    B. Rules and contracts are the basis for action, and decisions are made on an impersonal basis
    C. The right to give orders and instructions is inherent in the hierarchical arrangement of an organizational structure
    D. Realization that subordinates' needs for affiliation and recognition can contribute to management's objectives

    3.____

4. Of the following, the FIRST step in planning an operation is to
   A. obtain relevant information
   B. identify the goal to be achieved
   C. consider possible alternatives
   D. make necessary assignments

5. A supervisor who is extremely busy performing routine tasks is MOST likely making incorrect use of what basis principle of supervision?
   A. Homogeneous Assignment
   B. Span of Control
   C. Work Distribution
   D. Delegation of Authority

6. Controls help supervisors to obtain information from which they can determine whether their staffs are achieving planned goals.
   Which one of the following would be LEAST useful as a control device?
   A. Employee diaries
   B. Organization charts
   C. Periodic inspections
   D. Progress charts

7. A certain employee has difficulty in effectively performing a particular portion of his routine assignments, but his overall productivity is average.
   As a direct supervisor of this individual, your BEST course of action would be to
   A. attempt to develop the investigator's capacity to execute the problematical facets of his assignments
   B. diversify the investigator's work assignments in order to build up his confidence
   C. reassign the investigator to less difficult tasks
   D. request in a private conversation that the investigator improve his work output

8. A supervisor who uses persuasion as a means of supervising a unit would GENERALLY also use which of the following practices to supervise his unit?
   A. Supervises and control the staff with an authoritative attitude to indicate that he is a *take-charge* individual
   B. Make significant changes in the organizational operations so as to improve job efficiency
   C. Remove major communication barriers between himself, subordinates, and management
   D. Supervise everyday operations while being mindful of the problems of his subordinates

9. Whenever a supervisor in charge of a unit delegates a routine task to a capable subordinate, he tells him exactly how to do it.
   This practice is GENERALLY
   A. *desirable*, chiefly because good supervisors should be aware of the traits of their subordinates and delegate responsibilities to them accordingly
   B. *undesirable*, chiefly because only non-routine tasks should be delegated
   C. *desirable*, chiefly because a supervisor should frequently test the willingness of his subordinates to perform ordinary tasks
   D. *undesirable*, chiefly because a capable subordinate should usually be allowed to exercise his own discretion in doing a routine job

10. The one of the following activities through which a supervisor BEST demonstrates leadership ability is by
    A. arranging periodic staff meetings in order to keep his subordinates informed about professional developments in the field of investigation
    B. frequently issuing definite orders and directives which will lessen the need for subordinates to make decisions in handling any investigations assigned to them
    C. devoting the major part of his time to supervising subordinates so as to stimulate continuous improvement
    D. setting aside time for self-development and research so as to improve the investigative techniques and procedures of his unit

10.____

11. The following three statements relate to supervision of employees:
    I. The assignment of difficult tasks that offer a challenge is more conducive to good morale than the assignment of easy tasks.
    II. The same general principles of supervision that apply to men are equally applicable to women.
    III. The best restraining program should cover all phases of an employee's work in a general manner.
    Which of the following choices lists ALL of the above statements that are generally CORRECT?
    A. II, III   B. I   C. I, II   D. I, II, III

11.____

12. Which of the following examples BEST illustrates the application of the *exception principle* as a supervisory technique? A(n)
    A. complex job is divided among several employees who work simultaneously to complete the whole job in a shorter time
    B. employee is required to complete any task delegated to him to such an extent that nothing is left for the superior who delegated the task except to approve it
    C. superior delegates responsibility to a subordinate but retains authority to make the final decisions
    D. superior delegates all work possible to his subordinates and retains that which requires his personal attention or performance

12.____

13. Assume that you are a supervisor. Your immediate superior frequently gives orders to your subordinates without your knowledge.
    Of the following, the MOST direct and effective way for you to handle this problem is to
    A. tell your subordinates to take orders only from you
    B. submit a report to higher authority in which you cite specific instances
    C. discuss it with your immediate superior
    D. find out to what extent you authority and prestige as a supervisor have been affected

13.____

14. In an agency which has as its primary purpose the protection of the public against fraudulent business practices, which of the following would GENERALLY be considered an auxiliary or staff rather than a line function?

14.____

A. Interviewing victims of frauds and advising them about their legal remedies
B. Daily activities directed toward prevention of fraudulent business practices
C. Keeping records and statistics about business violations reported and corrected
D. Follow-up inspections by investigators after corrective action has been taken

15. A supervisor can MOST effectively reduce the spread of false rumors through the *grapevine* by
    A. identifying and disciplining any subordinate responsible for initiating such rumors
    B. keeping his subordinates informed as much as possible about matters affecting them
    C. denying false rumors which might tend to lower staff morale and productivity
    D. making sure confidential matters are kept secure from access by unauthorized employees

15.____

16. A supervisor has tried to learn about the background, education, and family relationships of his subordinates through observation, personal contact, and inspection of their personnel records.
    These supervisory actions are GENERALLY
    A. *inadvisable*, chiefly because they may lead to charges of favoritism
    B. *advisable*, chiefly because they may make him more popular with his subordinates
    C. *inadvisable*, chiefly because his efforts may be regarded as an invasion of privacy
    D. *advisable*, chiefly because the information may enable him to develop better understanding of each of his subordinates

16.____

17. In an emergency situation, when action must be taken immediately, it is BEST for the supervisor to give orders in the form of
    A. direct commands, which are brief and precise
    B. requests, so that his subordinate will not become alarmed
    C. suggestions, which offer alternative courses of action
    D. implied directive, so that his subordinates may use their judgment in carrying them out

17.____

18. When demonstrating a new and complex procedure to a group of subordinates, it is ESSENTIAL that a supervisor
    A. go slowly and repeat the steps involved at least once
    B. show the employees common errors and the consequences of such errors
    C. go through the process at the usual speed so that the employees can see the rate at which they should work
    D. distribute summaries of the procedure during the demonstration and instruct his subordinates to refer to them afterwards

18.____

19. The PRIMARY value of office reports and procedures is to 19.____
    A. assist top management in controlling key agency functions
    B. measure job performance
    C. save time and labor
    D. control the activities and use of time of all staff members

20. Of the following, which is considered to be the GREATEST advantage of the oral report? It 20.____
    A. allows for accurate transmission of information from one individual to another
    B. presents an opportunity to discuss or clarify any immediate questions raised by the receiver of the report
    C. requires less office work to maintain records on actions taken when an oral report is involved
    D. takes only a short amount of time to plan and prepare material for an oral report

21. A supervisor who is to make a report about a job he has done can make an oral report of a written report. 21.____
    Of the following, which is the BEST time to make an oral report? When
    A. the work covers an emergency situation
    B. a record is needed for the files
    C. the report is channeled to other departments
    D. the report covers additional work he will do

22. Suppose that a new employee has been assigned to you. It is your responsibility to see to it that he understands how to fill out properly the forms he is required to use. 22.____
    What would be the BEST way to do this?
    A. Explain the use of each form to the new technician and show him how to fill them out
    B. Give the new employee a copy of each form he must use so that he can learn by studying them
    C. Ask an experienced worker to explain clearly to him how the forms should be filled out
    D. Tell the new employee that filling out forms is simple and he should follow the instructions on each form

23. As a supervisor, you want to have your staff take part in improving work methods. 23.____
    Of the following, the BEST way to do this is to
    A. make critical appraisals of their work frequently
    B. encourage them to make suggestions
    C. make no change without their approval
    D. hold regular staff meetings

24. A good relationship with other supervisors is important to a senior supervisor. Close cooperation among supervisory personnel is MOST likely to result in
    A. increasing the probability for support of supervisory actions and decisions
    B. stimulating supervisors to achieve higher status in the organization
    C. helping to control the flow of work within a unit
    D. a clearer definition of the responsibilities of individual supervisors

25. Which of the following is MOST likely to gain a supervisor the respect and cooperation of his staff?
    A. Assigning the most difficult jobs to the experienced staff members
    B. Giving each staff member the same number of assignments
    C. Assigning jobs according to each staff member's ability
    D. Giving each staff member the same types of assignments

24.____

25.____

KEY (CORRECT ANSWERS)

1.	D		11.	C
2.	A		12.	D
3.	D		13.	C
4.	B		14.	C
5.	D		15.	B
6.	B		16.	D
7.	A		17.	A
8.	D		18.	A
9.	D		19.	A
10.	C		20.	B

21.	A
22.	A
23.	B
24.	A
25.	C

EXAMINATION SECTION
TEST 1

DIRECTIONS: Each question or incomplete statement is followed by several suggested answers or completions. Select the one that BEST answers the question or completes the statement. *PRINT THE LETTER OF THE CORRECT ANSWER IN THE SPACE AT THE RIGHT.*

1. Which one of the following is LEAST likely to be an area or cause of trouble in the use of staff personnel?

    A. Misunderstanding of the role the staff personnel are supposed to play as a result of vagueness of definition of their duties and authority
    B. Tendency of staff personnel almost always to be older than line personnel at comparable salary levels with whom they must deal
    C. Selection of staff personnel who fail to have simultaneously both competence in their specialities and skill in staff work
    D. The staff person fails to understand mixed staff and operating duties

2. Which of the following is generally NOT a valid statement with respect to the supervisory process?

    A. General supervision is more effective than close supervision.
    B. Employee-centered supervisors lead more effectively than do production-centered supervisors.
    C. Employee satisfaction is directly related to productivity.
    D. Low-producing supervisors use techniques that are different from high-producing supervisors.

3. Which of the following is the MOST essential element for proper evaluation of the performance of subordinate supervisors?

    A. Careful definition of each supervisor's specific job responsibilities and of his progress in meeting mutually agreed upon work goals
    B. System of rewards and penalties based on each supervisor's progress in meeting clearly defined performance standards
    C. Definition of personality traits, such as industry, initiative, dependability, and cooperativeness, required for effective job performance
    D. Breakdown of each supervisor's job into separate components and a rating of his performance on each individual task

4. The PRINCIPAL advantage of specialization for the operating efficiency of a public service agency is that specialization

    A. reduces the amount of red tape in coordinating the activities of mutually dependent departments
    B. simplifies the problem of developing adequate job controls
    C. provides employees with a clear understanding of the relationship of their activities to the overall objectives of the agency
    D. reduces destructive competition for power between departments

5. A list of conditions which encourages good morale inside a work group would NOT include a

   A. high rate of agreement among group members on values and objectives
   B. tight control system to minimize the risk of individual error
   C. good possibility that joint action will accomplish goals
   D. past history of successful group accomplishment

6. Of the following, the MOST important factor to be considered in selecting a training strategy or program is the

   A. requirements of the job to be performed by the trainees
   B. educational level or prior training of the trainees
   C. size of the training group
   D. quality and competence of available training specialists

7. Of the following, the one which is considered to be LEAST characteristic of the higher ranks of management is

   A. that higher levels of management benefit from modern technology
   B. that success is measured by the extent to which objectives are achieved
   C. the number of subordinates that directly report to a manager
   D. the de-emphasis of individual and specialized performance

8. Assume that a manager is preparing a training syllabus to be used in training members of her staff.
   Which of the following would NOT be a valid principle of the learning process to consider when preparing this training syllabus?

   A. When a person has thoroughly learned a task, it takes a lot of effort to create a little more improvement.
   B. In complicated learning situations, there is a period in which an additional period of practice produces an equal amount of improvement in learning.
   C. The less a person knows about the task, the slower the initial progress.
   D. The more a person knows about the task, the slower the initial progress.

9. Which statement BEST illustrates when collective bargaining agreements are working well?

   A. Executives strongly support subordinate managers.
   B. The management rights clause in the contract is clear and enforced.
   C. Contract provisions are competently interpreted.
   D. The provisions of the agreement are properly interpreted, communicated, and observed.

10. An executive who wishes to encourage subordinates to communicate freely with him about a job-related problem should FIRST

   A. state his own position on the problem before listening to the subordinates' ideas
   B. invite subordinates to give their own opinions on the problem
   C. ask subordinates for their reactions to his own ideas about the problem
   D. guard the confidentiality of management information about the problem

10._____

11. The ability to deal constructively with intra-organizational conflict is an essential attribute of the successful manager.
The one of the following types of conflict which would be LEAST difficult to handle constructively is a situation in which there is

   A. agreement on objectives, but disagreement as to the probable results of adopting the various alternatives
   B. agreement on objectives, disagreement on alternative courses of action, and relative certainty as to the outcome of one of the alternatives
   C. disagreement on objectives and on alternative courses of action, and relative certainty as to the outcome of one of the alternatives
   D. disagreement on objectives and on alternative courses of action, but uncertainty as to the outcome of the alternatives

11._____

12. Which of the following actions does NOT belong in a properly conducted grievance handling process?

   A. Gathering relevant information on why the grievance arose
   B. Formulating a personal judgment about the fairness or unfairness of the grievance at the time the grievance is presented
   C. Establishing tentative answers to the grievance
   D. Following up to see whether the solution has eliminated the difficulty

12._____

13. Grievances are generally defined as complaints expressed over work-related matters.
Which one of the following is MOST important for managers to be aware of in connection with this definition?
The

   A. fact that the definition fails to separate the subject of the grievance from the attitude of the grievant
   B. fact that anything in the organization may be the source of the grievance
   C. need to assume that dissatisfied people have adverse effects on productivity
   D. implication that management should be concerned about expressed grievances and unconcerned about unexpressed grievances

13._____

14. In carrying out disciplinary action, the MOST important procedure for all managers to follow is to

    A. convince all levels of management on the need for discipline from the organization's viewpoint
    B. follow up on a disciplinary action and not assume that the action has been effective
    C. convince all executives that proper discipline is a legitimate tool for their use
    D. convince all executives that they need to display confidence in the organization's rules

15. Assume that an employee under your supervision is acquitted in court of criminal charges arising out of his employment.
    Of the following statements concerning disciplinary action, which is MOST NEARLY correct?

    A. Disciplinary proceedings against the employee may not be held for the same offenses on which he was tried and acquitted.
    B. In a disciplinary action, the acquittal dispenses with the requirement that the employee be advised as to his constitutional rights.
    C. Civil Rights Law Section 79 prohibits the taking of any further punitive action by an employer if the offense did not involve official corruption.
    D. It is possible for the employee to be found guilty of the same offense when tried in a departmental hearing.

16. Work rules can be an effective tool in the process of personnel management.
    The BEST practical definition for work rules is that they are

    A. minimum standards of conduct or performance that apply to individuals or groups at work in an organization
    B. prescriptions that serve to specialize employee behavior
    C. predetermined decisions about disciplinary action
    D. the major determinant of an organization's climate and the morale of its workforce

Questions 17-18

DIRECTIONS: Questions 17 and 18 pertain to identification of words that are incorrectly used because they are not in keeping with the meaning of the quotation. In answering each question, the first step is to read the passage and identify the incorrectly used word, and then select the word which, when substituted, BEST serves to convey the meaning of the quotation.

17. Among the Housing Manager's overall responsibilities in administering a project is the prevention of the development of conditions which might lead to termination of tenancy and eviction of a tenant. Where there appears to be doubt that a tenant is fully aware of his responsibilities and is thus jeopardizing his tenancy, the Housing Manager should acquaint him with these responsibilities. Where a situation involves behavior of a tenant or a member of his family, the Housing Manager should confirm, through discussions and referrals to social agencies, correction of the conditions before they reach a state where there is no alternative but termination proceedings.

   A. Coordinate B. Identify
   C. Assert   D. Attempt

17._____

18. The one universal administrative complaint is that the budget is inadequate. Between adequacy and inadequacy lie all degrees of adequacy. Further, human wants are modest in relation to human resources. From these two facts we may conclude that the fundamental criterion of administrative decision must be a criterion of efficiency (the degree to which the goals have been reached relative to the available resources) rather than a criterion of adequacy (the degree to which its goals have been reached). The task of the manager is to maximize social values relative to limited resources.

   A. Improve   B. Simple
   C. Limitless D. Optimize

18._____

Questions 19-21.

DIRECTIONS: Questions 19 through 21 are to be answered SOLELY on the basis of the following situation.

John Foley, a top administrator, is responsible for output in his organization. Because productivity had been lagging for two periods in a row, Foley decided to establish a committee of his subordinate managers to investigate the reasons for the poor performance and to make recommendations for improvements. After two meetings, the committee came to the conclusions and made the recommendations that follow.

Output forecasts had been handed down from the top without prior consultation with middle management and first level supervision. Lines of authority and responsibility had been unclear. The planning and control process should be decentralized.

After receiving the committee's recommendations, Foley proceeded to take the following actions. Foley decided he would retain final authority to establish quotas but would delegate to the middle managers the responsibility for meeting quotas.

After receiving Foley's decision, the middle managers proceeded to delegate to the first-line supervisors the authority to establish their own quotas. The middle managers eventually received and combined the first-line supervisors' quotas so that these conformed to Foley's.

19. Foley's decision to delegate responsibility for meeting quotas to the middle managers is inconsistent with sound management principles because

    A. Foley should not have involved himself in the first place
    B. middle managers do not have the necessary skills
    C. quotas should be established by the chief executive
    D. responsibility should not be delegated

20. The principle of co-extensiveness of responsibility and authority bears on Foley's decision.
    In this case, it implies that

    A. authority should exceed responsibility
    B. authority should be delegated to match the degree of responsibility
    C. both authority and responsibility should be retained and not delegated
    D. responsibility should be delegated, but authority should be retained

21. The middle managers' decision to delegate to the first-line supervisors the authority to establish quotas was INCORRECTLY reasoned because

    A. delegation and control must go together
    B. first-line supervisors are in no position to establish quotas
    C. one cannot delegate authority that one does not possess
    D. the meeting of quotas should not be delegated

22. If one attempts to list the advantages of the management-by-exception principle as it is used in connection with the budgeting process, several distinct advantages could be cited.
    Which of the following is NOT an advantage of this principle as it applies to the budgeting process?
    Management-by-exception

    A. saves time
    B. identifies critical problem areas
    C. focuses attention and concentrates effort
    D. escalates the frequency and importance of budget-related decisions

23. The MOST accurate description of a budget is that

    A. a budget is made up by an organization to plan its future activities
    B. a budget specifies in dollars and cents how much is spent in a particular time period
    C. a budget specifies how much the organization to which it relates estimates it will spend over a certain period of time
    D. all plans dealing with money are budgets

24. Of the following, the one which is NOT a contribution that a budget makes to organizational programming is that a budget

   A. enables a comparison of what actually happened with what was expected
   B. stresses the need to forecast specific goals and eliminates the need to focus on tasks needed to accomplish goals
   C. may illustrate duplication of effort between interdependent activities
   D. shows the relationship between various organizational segments

25. A line-item budget is a good control budget because

   A. it clearly specifies how the items being purchased will be used
   B. expenditures can be shown primarily for contractual services
   C. it clearly specifies what the money is buying
   D. it clearly specifies the services to be provided

KEY (CORRECT ANSWERS)

1. B
2. C
3. A
4. B
5. B

6. A
7. A
8. D
9. D
10. B

11. B
12. B
13. C
14. B
15. D

16. A
17. D
18. C
19. D
20. B

21. C
22. D
23. C
24. B
25. C

TEST 2

DIRECTIONS: Each question or incomplete statement is followed by several suggested answers or completions. Select the one that BEST answers the question or completes the statement. *PRINT THE LETTER OF THE CORRECT ANSWER IN THE SPACE AT THE RIGHT.*

1. The insights of Chester I. Barnard have influenced the development of management thought in significant ways. He is MOST closely identified with a position that has become known as the

    A. acceptance theory of authority
    B. principle of the manager's or executive's span of control
    C. *Theory X* and *Theory Y* dichotomy
    D. unit of command principle

    1._____

2. Certain conditions should exist to insure that a subordinate will decide to accept a communication as being authoritative.
   Which of the following is LEAST valid as a condition which should exist?

    A. The subordinate understands the communication.
    B. At the time of the subordinate's decision, he views the communication as consistent with the organization's purpose and his personal interest.
    C. At the time of the subordinate's decision, he views the communication as more consistent with his personal purposes than with the organization's interest.
    D. The subordinate is mentally and physically able to comply with the communication.

    2._____

3. In exploring the effects that employee participation has on implementing changes in work methods, certain relationships have been established between participation and productivity.
   It has MOST generally been found that highest productivity occurs in groups provided with

    A. participation in the process of change only through representatives of their group
    B. no participation in the change process
    C. full participation in the change process
    D. intermittent participation in the process of change

    3._____

4. The trend LEAST likely to occur in the area of employee-management relations is that

    A. employees will exert more influence on decisions affecting their interests
    B. technological change will have a stronger impact on organizations' human resources
    C. labor will judge management according to company profits
    D. government will play a larger role in balancing the interests of the parties in labor-management affairs

    4._____

5. Members of an organization must satisfy several fundamental psychological needs in order to be happy and productive.
The BROADEST and MOST basic needs are

   A. achievement, recognition, and acceptance
   B. competition, recognition, and accomplishment
   C. salary increments and recognition
   D. acceptance of competition and economic award

6. Morale has been defined as the capacity of a group of people to pull together steadily for a common purpose.
Morale thus defined is MOST generally dependent on

   A. job security
   B. group and individual self-confidence
   C. organizational efficiency
   D. physical health of the individuals

7. Which is the CORRECT order of steps to follow when revising office procedure?
To

   I. develop the improved method as determined by time and motion studies and effective workplace layout
   II. find out how the task is now performed
   III. apply the new method
   IV. analyze the current method

   The CORRECT answer is:
   A. IV, II, I, III
   B. II, I, III, IV
   C. I, II, IV, III
   D. II, IV, I, III

8. In contrast to broad spans of control, narrow spans of control are MOST likely to

   A. provide opportunity for more personal contact between superior and subordinate
   B. encourage decentralization
   C. stress individual initiative
   D. foster group of team effort

9. A manager is coaching a subordinate on the nature of decision-making. She could BEST define decision-making as

   A. choosing between alternatives
   B. making diagnoses of feasible ends
   C. making diagnoses of feasible means
   D. comparing alternatives

10. Of the following, the LEAST valid purpose of an organizational policy statement is to

    A. keep personnel from performing improper actions and functions on routine matters
    B. prevent the mishandling of non-routine matters
    C. provide management personnel with a tool that precludes the need for their use of judgment
    D. provide standard decisions and approaches in handling problems of a recurrent nature

11. Current thinking on bureaucratic organizations is that

    A. bureaucracy is on the way out
    B. bureaucracy, though not perfect, is unlikely to be replaced
    C. bureaucratic organizations are most effective in dealing with constant change
    D. bureaucratic organizations are most effective when dealing with sophisticated customers or clients

12. The development of alternate plans as a major step in planning will normally result in the planner's having several possible course of action available. GENERALLY, this is

    A. *desirable* since such development helps to determine the most suitable alternative and to provide for the unexpected
    B. *desirable* since such development makes the use of planning premises and constraints unnecessary
    C. *undesirable* since the planners should formulate only one way of achieving given goals at a given time
    D. *undesirable* since such action restricts efforts to modify the planning to take advantage of opportunities

13. Assume a manager carries out his responsibilities to his staff according to what is now known about managerial leadership.
    Which of the following statements would MOST accurately reflect his assumptions about proper management?

    A. Efficiency in operations results from allowing the human element to participate in a minimal way.
    B. Efficient operation results from balancing work considerations with personnel considerations.
    C. Efficient operation results from a work force committed to its self-interest.
    D. Efficient operation results from staff relationships that produce a friendly work climate.

14. Assume that a manager is called upon to conduct a management audit. To do this properly, he would have to take certain steps in a specific sequence. Which step should this manager take FIRST?

    A. Managerial performance must be surveyed.
    B. A method of reporting must be established.
    C. Management auditing procedures and documentation must be developed.
    D. Criteria for the audit must be established.

14._____

15. If a manager is required to conduct a scientific investigation of an organizational problem, the FIRST step he should take is to

    A. state his assumptions about the problem
    B. carry out a search for background information
    C. choose the right approach to investigate the validity of his assumptions
    D. define and state the problem

15._____

16. A manager would be correct to assert that the principle of delegation states that decisions should be made PRIMARILY

    A. by persons in an executive capacity qualified to make them
    B. by persons in a non-executive capacity
    C. at as low an organizational level of authority as practicable
    D. by the next lower level of authority

16._____

17. Of the following, which one is NOT regarded by management authorities as a fundamental characteristic of an ideal bureaucracy?

    A. Division of labor and specialization
    B. An established hierarchy
    C. Decentralization of authority
    D. A set of operating rules and regulations

17._____

18. As the number of subordinates in a manager's span of control increases, the actual number of possible relationships

    A. increases disproportionately to the number of subordinates
    B. increases in equal number to the number of subordinates
    C. reaches a stable level
    D. will first increase, then slowly decrease

18._____

19. Management experts generally believe that computer-based management information systems (MIS) have greater potential for improving the process of management than any other development in recent decades.
The one of the following which MOST accurately describes the objectives of MIS is to

   A. provide information for decision-making on planning, initiating, and controlling the operations of the various units of the organization
   B. establish mechanization of routine functions such as clerical records, payroll, inventory, and accounts receivable in order to promote economy and efficiency
   C. computerize decision-making on planning, initiating, organizing, and controlling the operations of an organization
   D. provide accurate facts and figures on the various programs of the organization to be used for purposes of planning and research

19._____

20. The one of the following which is the BEST application of the *management-by-exception* principle is that this principle

   A. stimulates communication and aids in management of crisis situations, thus reducing the frequency of decision-making
   B. saves time and reserves top management decisions only for crisis situations, thus reducing the frequency of decision-making
   C. stimulates communication, saves time, and reduces the frequency of decision-making
   D. is limited to crisis-management situations

20._____

21. Generally, each organization is dependent upon the availability of qualified personnel.
Of the following, the MOST important factor affecting the availability of qualified people to each organization is

   A. availability of public transportation
   B. the general rise in the educational levels of our population
   C. the rise of sentiment against racial discrimination
   D. pressure by organized community groups

21._____

22. A fundamental responsibility of all managers is to decide what physical facilities and equipment are needed to help attain basic goals.
Good planning for the purchase and use of equipment is seldom easy to do and is complicated most by the fact that

   A. organizations rarely have stable sources of supply
   B. nearly all managers tend to be better at personnel planning than at equipment planning
   C. decisions concerning physical resources are made too often on an emergency basis rather than under carefully prepared policies
   D. legal rulings relative to depreciation fluctuate very frequently

22._____

23. In attempting to reconcile managerial objectives and an individual employee's goals, it is generally LEAST desirable for management to

    A. recognize the capacity of the individual to contribute toward realization of managerial goals
    B. encourage self-development of the employee to exceed minimum job performance
    C. consider an individual employee's work separately from other employees
    D. demonstrate that an employee advances only to the extent that he contributes directly to the accomplishment of stated goals

24. As a management tool for discovering individual training needs, a job analysis would generally be of LEAST assistance in determining

    A. the performance requirements of individual jobs
    B. actual employee performance on the job
    C. acceptable standards of performance
    D. training needs for individual jobs

25. One of the major concerns of organizational managers today is how the spread of automation will affect them and the status of their positions. Realistically speaking, one can say that the MOST likely effect of our newer forms of highly automated technology on managers will be to

    A. make most top-level positions superfluous or obsolete
    B. reduce the importance of managerial work in general
    C. replace the work of managers with the work of technicians
    D. increase the importance of and demand for top managerial personnel

KEY (CORRECT ANSWERS)

1. A
2. C
3. C
4. C
5. A

6. B
7. D
8. A
9. A
10. C

11. B
12. A
13. B
14. D
15. D

16. C
17. C
18. A
19. A
20. C

21. B
22. C
23. C
24. B
25. D

READING COMPREHENSION
UNDERSTANDING AND INTERPRETING WRITTEN MATERIAL
EXAMINATION SECTION
TEST 1

DIRECTIONS: Each question or incomplete statement is followed by several suggested answers or completions. Select the one that BEST answers the question or completes the statement. *PRINT THE LETTER OF THE CORRECT ANSWER IN THE SPACE AT THE RIGHT.*

Questions 1-3.

DIRECTIONS: Questions 1 through 3 are to be answered SOLELY on the basis of the following paragraph.

The aging housing inventory presents a broad spectrum of conditions, from good upkeep to unbelievable deterioration. Buildings, even relatively good buildings, are likely to have numerous minor violations rather than the gross and evident sanitary violations of an earlier age. Except for the serious violations in a relatively small number of slum buildings, the task is to deal with masses of minor violations that, though insignificant in themselves, amount in the aggregate to major deprivations of health and comfort to tenants. Caused by wear and tear, by the abrasions of time, and aggravated by neglect, these conditions do not readily yield to the dramatic *vacate and restore* measures of earlier times. Moreover, the lines between *good* and *bad* housing have become blurred in many parts of our cities; we find a range of *shades of gray* blending into each other. Different kinds of code enforcement efforts may be required to deal with different degrees of deterioration.

1. The above passage suggests that code enforcement efforts may have to be

    A. developed to cope with varying levels of housing dilapidation
    B. aimed primarily at the serious violations in slum buildings
    C. modeled on the *vacate and restore* measures of earlier times
    D. modified to reduce unrealistic penalties for petty violations

1.____

2. According to the above passage, during former times some buildings had sanitary violations which were

    A. irreparable and minor
    B. blurred and gray
    C. flagrant and obvious
    D. insignificant and numerous

2.____

3. According to the above passage, the aging housing stock presents a

    A. great number of rent-controlled buildings
    B. serious problem of tenant-caused deterioration
    C. significant increase in buildings without intentional violations
    D. wide range of physical conditions

3.____

Questions 4-5.

DIRECTIONS: Questions 4 and 5 are to be answered SOLELY on the basis of the following passage.

In general, housing code provisions relating to the safe and sanitary maintenance of dwelling units prescribe the maintenance required for foundations, walls, ceilings, floors, windows, doors, stairways, and also the facilities and equipment required in other sections. The more recent codes have, in addition, extensive provisions designed to ensure that the unit be maintained in a rat-free and rat-proof condition. Also, as an example of new approaches in code provisions, one proposed Federal model housing code prohibits the landlord from terminating vital services and utilities except during temporary emergencies or when actual repairs or maintenance are in process. This provision may be used to prevent a landlord from turning off utility services as a technique of self-help eviction or as a weapon against rent strikes.

4. According to the above passage, the more recent housing codes have extensive provisions designed to   4.____

   A. maintain a reasonably fire-proof living unit
   B. prohibit tenants from participating in rent strikes
   C. maintain the unit free from rats
   D. prohibit tenants from using lead-based paints

5. According to the above passage, one housing code would permit landlords to terminate vital services during   5.____

   A. a rent strike
   B. an actual eviction
   C. a temporary emergency
   D. the planning of repairs and maintenance

Questions 6-8.

DIRECTIONS: Questions 6 through 8 are to be answered SOLELY on the basis of the following passage.

City governments have long had building codes which set minimum standards for building and for human occupancy. The code (or series of codes) makes provisions for standards of lighting and ventilation, sanitation, fire prevention, and protection. As a result of demands from manufacturers, builders, real estate people, tenement owners, and building-trades unions, these codes often have established minimum standards well below those that the contemporary society would accept as a rock-bottom minimum. Codes often become outdated so that meager standards in one era become seriously inadequate a few decades later as society"s concept of a minimum standard of living changes. Out-of-date codes, when still in use, have sometimes prevented the introduction of new devices and modern building techniques. Thus, it is extremely important that building codes keep pace with changes in the accepted concept of a minimum standard of living.

6. According to the above passage, all of the following considerations in building planning would probably be covered in a building code EXCEPT

   A. closet space as a percentage of total floor area
   B. size and number of windows required for rooms of differing sizes
   C. placement of fire escapes in each line of apartments
   D. type of garbage disposal units to be installed

7. According to the above passage, if an ideal building code were to be created, how would the established minimum standards in it compare to the ones that are presently set by city governments?
   They would

   A. be lower than they are at present
   B. be higher than they are at present
   C. be comparable to the present minimum standards
   D. vary according to the economic group that sets them

8. On the basis of the above passage, what is the reason for difficulties in introducing new building techniques?

   A. Builders prefer techniques which represent the rock-bottom minimum desired by society.
   B. Certain manufacturers have obtained patents on various building methods to the exclusion of new techniques.
   C. The government does not want to invest money in techniques that will soon be outdated.
   D. New techniques are not provided for in building codes which are not up-to-date.

Questions 9-11.

DIRECTIONS: Questions 9 through 11 are to be answered SOLELY on the basis of the following paragraph.

When constructed within a multiple dwelling, such storage space shall be equipped with a sprinkler system and also with a system of mechanical ventilation in no way connected with any other ventilating system. Such storage space shall have no opening into any other part of the dwelling except through a fireproof vestibule. Any such vestibule shall have a minimum superficial floor area of fifty square feet, and its maximum area shall not exceed seventy-five square feet. It shall be enclosed with incombustible partitions having a fire-resistive rating of three hours. The floor and ceiling of such vestibule shall also be of incombustible material having a fire-resistive rating of at least three hours. There shall be two doors to provide access from the dwelling,to the car storage space. Each such door shall have a fire-resistive rating of one and one-half hours and shall be provided with a device to prevent the opening of one door until the other door is entirely closed.

9. According to the above paragraph, the one of the following that is REQUIRED in order for cars to be permitted to be stored in a multiple dwelling is a(n)

   A. fireproof vestibule
   B. elevator from the garage
   C. approved heating system
   D. sprinkler system

10. According to the above paragraph, the one of the following materials that would NOT be acceptable for the walls of a vestibule connecting a garage to the dwelling portion of a building is

    A. 3" solid gypsum blocks
    B. 4" brick
    C. 4" hollow gypsum blocks, plastered both sides
    D. 6" solid cinder concrete blocks

11. According to the above paragraph, the one of the following that would be ACCEPTABLE for the width and length of a vestibule connecting a garage that is within a multiple dwelling to the dwelling portion of the building is

    A. 3'8" x 13'0"
    B. 4'6" x 18'6"
    C. 4'9" x 14'6"
    D. 4'3" x 19'3"

Questions 12-13.

DIRECTIONS: Questions 12 and 13 are to be answered SOLELY on the basis of the following paragraph.

It shall be unlawful to place, use, or maintain in a condition intended, arranged, or designed for use, any gas-fired cooking appliance, laundry stove, heating stove, range or water heater or combination of such appliances in any room or space used for living or sleeping in any new or existing multiple dwelling unless such room or space has a window opening to the outer air or such gas appliance is vented to the outer air. All automatically operated gas appliances shall be equipped with a device which shall shut off automatically the gas supply to the main burners when the pilot light in such appliance is extinguished. A gas range or the cooking portion of a gas appliance incorporating a room heater shall not be deemed an automatically operated gas appliance. However, burners in gas ovens and broilers which can be turned on and off or ignited by non-manual means shall be equipped with a device which shall shut off automatically the gas supply to those burners when the operation of such non-manual means fails.

12. According to the above paragraph, an automatic shut-off device is NOT required on a gas

    A. hot water heater
    B. laundry dryer
    C. space heater
    D. range

13. According to the above paragraph, a gas-fired water heater is permitted

    A. only in kitchens
    B. only in bathrooms
    C. only in living rooms
    D. in any type of room

Questions 14-18.

DIRECTIONS: Questions 14 through 18 are to be answered SOLELY on the basis of the information contained in the statement below.

No multiple dwelling shall be erected to a height in excess of one and one-half times the width of the widest street on which it faces, except that above the level of such height, for each one foot that the front wall of such dwelling sets back from the street line, three feet shall be added to the height limit of such dwelling, but such dwelling shall not exceed in maximum height three feet plus one and three-quarter times the width of the widest street on which it faces.

Any such dwelling facing a street more than one hundred feet in width shall be subject to the same height limitations as though such dwelling faced a street one hundred feet in width.

14. The MAXIMUM height of a multiple dwelling set back five feet from the street line and facing a 60 foot wide street is ___ feet.

    A. 60   B. 90   C. 105   D. 165

15. The MAXIMUM height of a multiple dwelling set back six feet from the street line and facing a 120 foot wide street is ___ feet.

    A. 198   B. 168   C. 120   D. 105

16. The MAXIMUM height of a multiple dwelling is

    A. 100 ft.   B. 150 ft.   C. 178 ft.   D. unlimited

17. The MAXIMUM height of a multiple dwelling set back 10 feet from the street line and facing a 110 foot wide street is ___ feet.

    A. 178   B. 180   C. 195   D. 205

18. The MAXIMUM height of a multiple dwelling set back eight feet from the street line and facing a 90 foot wide street is ___ feet.

    A. 135   B. 147   C. 178   D. 159

Questions 19-23.

DIRECTIONS: Questions 19 through 23 are to be answered SOLELY on the basis of the following statement.

The number of persons accommodated on any story in a lodging house shall not be greater than the sum of the following components,

   a. 22 persons for each full multiple of 22 inches in the smallest clear width for each means of egress approved by the department, other than fire escapes
   b. 20 persons for each lawful fire escape accessible from such story.

19. The MAXIMUM number of persons that may be accommodated on a story in a lodging house depends on the

    A. number of lawful fire escapes *only*
    B. number of approved means of egress *only*
    C. smallest clear width in each approved means of egress *only*
    D. number of lawful fire escapes and sum total of smallest clear widths in each approved means of egress

20. The MAXIMUM number of persons that may be accommodated on a story of a lodging house having one lawful fire escape and a sum total of 44 inches in the smallest clear widths of the two approved means of egress is

    A. 20   B. 22   C. 42   D. 64

21. The MAXIMUM number of persons that may be accommodated on a story of a lodging house having two lawful fire escapes and a sum total of 60 inches in the smallest clear width of the approved means of egress is

    A. 64   B. 84   C. 100   D. 106

22. The MAXIMUM number of persons that may be accommodated on a story of a lodging house having one lawful fire escape and a sum total of 33 inches in the smallest clear width of the approved means of egress is

    A. 42   B. 53   C. 64   D. 73

23. The MAXIMUM number of persons that may be accommodated on a story of a lodging house having two lawful fire escapes and two approved means of egress, with 40 inches and 44 inches in the smallest clear widths, respectively, is

    A. 84   B. 104   C. 106   D. 108

Questions 24-25.

DIRECTIONS: Questions 24 and 25 are to be answered SOLELY on the basis of the following paragraph.

Though the recent trend toward apartment construction may appear to be the Region's response to large-lot zoning and centralized industry, it really is not. It is mainly a function of the age of the population. Most of the apartments are occupied by one- and two-person families young people out of school but without a family of their own and older people whose children have grown. Both groups have been increasing in number; and, in this Region, they characteristically live in apartments. It is this increased demand for apartments and the simultaneous decrease in demand for one-family houses that dramatically raised the percentage of building permits issued for multi-family housing units from 36 percent in 1977 to 67 percent in 1981. The fact that three-fourths of the apartments were built in the Core between 1977 and 1981 at the same time as the Core was losing population underscores the failure of the apartment boom to slow the outward spread of the population.

24. According to the above paragraph, one of the reasons for the increase in the number of building permits issued for multi-family construction in the City Metropolitan Region is

    A. that workers in industry want to live close to their jobs
    B. an increase in the number of elderly people living in the Region
    C. the inability of many families to afford the large lots necessary to build private homes
    D. the new zoning ordinance made it easier to build apartments

25. According to the above paragraph, the apartment construction boom

    A. increased the population density in the Core
    B. spurred a population shift to the suburbs
    C. did not halt the outward flow of the population from the Core
    D. was most significant in the outer areas of the Region

KEY (CORRECT ANSWERS)

1. A
2. C
3. D
4. C
5. C

6. A
7. B
8. D
9. D
10. B

11. C
12. D
13. D
14. C
15. B

16. C
17. A
18. D
19. D
20. D

21. B
22. A
23. C
24. B
25. C

TEST 2

DIRECTIONS: Each question or incomplete statement is followed by several suggested answers or completions. Select the one that BEST answers the question or completes the statement. *PRINT THE LETTER OF THE CORRECT ANSWER IN THE SPACE AT THE RIGHT.*

Questions 1-4.

DIRECTIONS: Questions 1 through 4 are to be answered SOLELY on the basis of the following paragraph.

Although the suburbs have provided housing and employment for millions of additional families since 1950, many suburban communities have maintained controls over the kinds of families who can live in them. Suburban attitudes have been formed by reaction against a perception of crowded, harassed city life and threatening alien city people. As population, taxable income, and jobs have left the cities for the suburbs, the *urban crisis* of substandard housing, declining levels of education and public services, and decreasing employment opportunities has been created. The crisis, however, is not urban at all, but national, and in part a result of the suburban policy that discourages outward movement by the urban poor.

1. According to the above paragraph, the quality of urban life

    A. is determined by public opinion in the cities
    B. has worsened in recent years
    C. is similar to rural life
    D. can be changed by political means

1.____

2. According to the above paragraph, suburban communities have

    A. tried to show that the urban crisis is really a national crisis
    B. avoided taking a position on the urban crisis
    C. been involved in causing the urban crisis
    D. been the innocent victims of the urban crisis

2.____

3. According to the above paragraph, the poor have

    A. become increasingly sophisticated in their attempts to move to the suburbs
    B. generally been excluded from the suburbs
    C. lost incentive for betterment of their living conditions
    D. sought improvement of the central cities

3.____

4. As used in the above paragraph, the word perception means MOST NEARLY

    A. development
    B. impression
    C. opposition
    D. uncertainty

4.____

Questions 5-8.

DIRECTIONS: Questions 5 through 8 are to be answered SOLELY on the basis of the following paragraph.

The concentration of publicly assisted housing in central cities -- because the suburbs do not want them and effectively bar them -- is usually rationalized by a solicitous regard for keeping intact the city neighborhoods cherished by low-income groups. If one accepted this as valid, the devotion of minorities to blighted city neighborhoods in preference to suburban employment and housing would be an historic first. Certainly no such devotion was visible among the millions who have deserted their city neighborhoods in the last 25 years even if it meant an arduous daily trip from the suburbs to their jobs in the cities.

5. The writer implies that MOST poor people

   A. prefer isolation
   B. fear change
   C. are angry
   D. seek betterment

6. The general tone of the paragraph is BEST characterized as

   A. uncertain   B. skeptical   C. evasive   D. indifferent

7. As used in the above paragraph, the word <u>rationalize</u> means MOST NEARLY

   A. dispute   B. justify   C. deny   D. locate

8. According to the above paragraph, publicly assisted housing is concentrated in the central cities PRIMARILY because

   A. city dwellers are unable to find satisfactory housing
   B. deterioration of older housing has increased in recent years
   C. suburbanites have opposed the movement of the poor to the suburbs
   D. employment opportunities have decreased in the suburbs

Questions 9-11.

DIRECTIONS: Questions 9 through 11 are to be answered SOLELY on the basis of the following paragraph.

In recent years, new and important emphasis has been placed upon the maximum use of conservation and rehabilitation techniques in carrying out programs of urban renewal and revitalization. In urban renewal projects where existing structures are hopelessly deteriorated or land uses are incompatible with the community's overall plans, the entire area may be acquired, cleared, and sold for redevelopment. However, where existing structures are basically sound but have deteriorated to the point where they are a <u>blighting</u> influence on the neighborhood, they may be salvaged through a program of rehabilitation and reconditioning.

9. According to the above paragraph, the one of the following which is MOST likely to cause area-wide razing of the buildings in urban renewal programs is

   A. a program of rehabilitation and reconditioning
   B. concerted insistence by landlords and tenants that certain buildings be bulldozed
   C. an inability of community groups to agree on priorities for staged clearance
   D. land use contrary to the community's general plan

10. According to the above paragraph, rehabilitation of structures may take place if

    A. new conservation and rehabilitation techniques are used
    B. salvaging all the buildings in the entire area is hopeless
    C. the community wishes to preserve historic structures
    D. the existing buildings are structurally sound

11. As used in the above paragraph, the word <u>blighting</u> means MOST NEARLY 11._____

    A. ruining   B. infrequent   C. recurrent   D. traditional

Questions 12-13.

DIRECTIONS: Questions 12 and 13 are to be answered SOLELY on the basis of the following paragraphs.

    We must also find better ways to handle the relocation of people uprooted by projects. In the past, many renewal plans have foundered on this problem, and it is still the most difficult part of the community development. Large-scale replacement of low-income residents -- many ineligible for public housing -- has contributed to deterioration of surrounding communities. However, thanks to changes in housing authority procedures, relocation has been accomplished in a far more satisfactory fashion. The step-by-step community development projects we advocate in this plan should bring further improvement.

    But additional measures will be necessary. There are going to be more people to be moved; and, with the current shortage of apartments, large ones especially, it is going to be tougher to find places to move them to. The city should have more freedom to buy or lease housing that comes on the market because of normal turnover and make it available to relocatees.

12. According to the above paragraphs, one of the reasons a neighborhood may deteriorate is that 12._____

    A. there is a scarcity of large apartments
    B. step-by-step community development projects have failed
    C. people in the given neighborhood are uprooted from their homes
    D. a nearby renewal project has an inadequate relocation plan

13. From the above paragraphs, one might conclude that the relocation phase of community renewal has been improved. 13._____

    A. by changes in housing authority procedures
    B. by development of step-by-step community development projects
    C. through expanded city powers to buy housing for relocation
    D. by the addition of huge sums of money

Questions 14-15.

DIRECTIONS: Questions 14 and 15 are to be answered SOLELY on the basis of the following paragraphs.

    Provision of decent housing for the lower half of the population (by income) was thus taken on as a public responsibility. Public housing was to assist the poorest quarter of urban families while the 221(d)(3) Housing Program would assist the next quarter. But limited funds meant that the supply of subsidized housing could not stretch nearly far enough to help this half of the population. Who were to be left out in the rationing process which was accomplished by the sifting of applicants for housing on the part of public and private authorities?

Discrimination on the grounds of race or color is not allowed under Federal law. In all sections of the country, encouragingly, housing programs are found which follow this law to the letter. Yet, housing programs in some cities still suffer from the residue of racial segregation policies and attitudes that for years were condoned or even encouraged.

Some sifting in the 221(d)(3) Housing Program follows the practice of many public housing authorities, the imposition of requirements with respect to character. This is a delicate matter. To fill a project overwhelmingly with broken families, alcoholics, criminals, delinquents, and other problem tenants would hardly make it a wholesome environment. Yet the total exclusion of such families is hardly an acceptable alternative. To the extent this exclusion is practiced, the very people whose lives are described in order to persuade lawmakers and the public to instigate new programs find the door shut in their faces when such programs come into being. The proper balance is difficult to achieve, but society's neediest families surely should not be totally denied the opportunities for rejuvenation in subsidized housing.

14. From the above paragraphs, it can be assumed that the 221(d)(3) Housing Program

    A. served a population earning more than the median income
    B. served a less affluent population than is served by public housing
    C. excludes all problem families from its projects
    D. is a subsidized housing program

15. According to this text, the provision of housing for the poor

    A. has not been completely accomplished with public monies
    B. is never influenced by segregationist policies
    C. is limited to providing housing for only the neediest families
    D. is primarily the responsibility of the Federal government

16. Five hundred persons attended a public hearing at which a proposed public housing project was being considered. Less than half favored the project while the majority opposed the project.
    According to the above statement, it is REASONABLE to conclude that

    A. the proposal stimulated considerable community interest
    B. the public housing project was disapproved by the city because a majority opposed it
    C. those who opposed the project lacked sympathy for needy persons
    D. the supporters of the project were led by militants

17. A vacant lot close to a polluted creek is for sale. Two buyers compete. One owns an adjacent factory which provides 300 high paying unskilled jobs. He needs to expand or move from the city. If he expands, he will provide 300 additional jobs. The other is a community group in a changing residential area close by. They hope to stabilize the neighborhood by bringing in new housing. They would build an apartment building with 100 dwelling units on the lot.
    According to the above paragraph, it is REASONABLE to conclude that

    A. jobs are more important than housing
    B. there is conflict between the factory owners and the neighborhood group
    C. the neighborhood group will not succeed in stabilizing the area by constructing new housing
    D. the polluted creek should be cleaned up

18. The housing authority faces every problem of the private developer, and it must also assume responsibilities of which private building is free. The authority must account to the community; it must conform to federal regulations; it must provide durable buildings of good standard at low cost; it must overcome the prejudices against public operations, of contractors, bankers, and prospective tenants. These authorities are being watched by anti-housing enthusiasts for the first error of judgment or the first evidence of high costs, to be torn to bits before a Congressional committee.
On the basis of this statement, it would be MOST correct to state that

   A. private builders do not have the opposition of contractors, bankers, and prospective tenants
   B. Congressional committees impede the progress of public housing by petty investigations
   C. a housing authority must deal with all the difficulties encountered by the private builder
   D. housing authorities are no more immune from errors in judgment than private developers

19. Another factor that has considerably added to the city's housing crisis has been the great influx of low-income workers and their families seeking better employment opportunities during wartime and defense boom periods. The circumstances of these families have forced them to crowd into the worst kind of housing and have produced on a renewed scale the conditions from which slums flourish and grow.
On the basis of this statement, one would be justified in stating that

   A. the influx of low-income workers has aggravated the slum problem
   B. the city has better employment opportunities than other sections of the country
   C. the high wages paid by our defense industries have made many families ineligible for tenancy in public housing projects
   D. the families who settled in the city during wartime and the defense build-up brought with them language and social customs conducive to the growth of slums

20. Much of the city felt the effects of the general postwar increase of vandalism and street crime, and the greatly expanded public housing program was no exception. Projects built in congested slum areas with a high incidence of delinquency and crime were particularly subjected to the depredations of neighborhood gangs. The civil service watchmen who patrolled the projects, unarmed and neither trained nor expected to perform police duties, were unable to cope with the situation.
On the basis of this statement, the MOST accurate of the following statements is:

   A. Neighborhood gangs were particularly responsible for the high incidence of delinquency and crime in congested slum areas having public housing programs
   B. Civil service watchmen who patrolled housing projects failed to carry out their assigned police duties
   C. Housing projects were not spared the effects of the general postwar increase of vandalism and street crime
   D. Delinquency and crime affected housing projects in slum areas to a greater extent than other dwellings in the same area

21. Another peculiar characteristic of real estate is the absence of liquidity. Each parcel is a discrete unit as to size, location, rental, physical condition, and financing arrangements. Each property requires investigation, comparison of rents with other properties, and individualized haggling on price and terms.
On the basis of this statement, the LEAST accurate of the following statements is:

    A. Although the size, location, and rent of parcels vary, comparison with rents of other properties affords an indication of the value of a particular parcel
    B. Bargaining skill is the essential factor in determining the value of a parcel of real estate
    C. Each parcel of real estate has individual peculiarities distinguishing it from any other parcel
    D. Real estate is not easily converted to other types of assets

21._____

22. In part, at least, the charges of sameness, monotony, and institutionalism directed at public housing projects result from the degree in which they differ from the city's normal housing pattern. They seem alike because their very difference from the usual makes them stand apart.
In many respects, there is considerably more variety between public housing projects than there is between different streets of apartment houses or tenements throughout the city.
On the basis of this statement, it would be LEAST accurate to state that:

    A. There is considerably more variety between public housing projects than there is between different streets of tenements throughout the city
    B. Public housing projects differ from the city's normal housing pattern to the degree that sameness, monotony, and institutionalism are characteristic of public buildings
    C. Public housing projects seem alike because their deviation from the usual dwellings draws attention to them
    D. The variety in structure between public housing projects and other public buildings is related to the period in which they were built

22._____

23. The amount of debt that can be charged against the city for public housing is limited by law. Part of the city's restricted housing means goes for cash subsidies it may be required to contribute to state-aided projects. Under the provisions of the state law, the city must match the state's contributions in subsidies; and while the value of the partial tax exemption granted by the city is counted for this purpose, it is not always sufficient.
On the basis of this statement, it would be MOST accurate to state that:

    A. The amount of money the city may spend for public housing is limited by annual tax revenues
    B. The value of tax exemptions granted by the city to educational, religious, and charitable institutions may be added to its subsidy contributions to public housing projects
    C. The subsidy contributions for state-aided public housing projects are shared equally by the state and the city under the provisions of the state law
    D. The tax revenues of the city, unless supplemented by state aid, are insufficient to finance public housing projects

23._____

24. Maintenance costs can be minimized and the useful life of houses can be extended by building with the best and most permanent materials available. The best and most permanent materials in many cases are, however, much more expensive than materials which require more maintenance. The most economical procedure in home building has been to compromise between the capital costs of high quality and enduring materials and the maintenance costs of less desirable materials.
On the basis of this statement, one would be justified in stating that:

   A. Savings in maintenance costs make the use of less durable and less expensive building materials preferable to high quality materials that would prolong the useful life of houses constructed from them
   B. Financial advantage can be secured by the home builder if he judiciously combines costly but enduring building materials with less desirable materials which, however, require more maintenance
   C. A compromise between the capital costs of high quality materials and the maintenance costs of less desirable materials makes it easier for a home builder to estimate construction expenditures
   D. The most economical procedure in home building is to balance the capital costs of the most permanent materials against the costs of less expensive materials that are cheaper to maintain

25. Personnel selection has been a critical problem for local housing authorities. The pool of qualified workers trained in housing procedures is small, and the colleges and universities have failed to grasp the opportunity for enlarging it. While real estate experience makes a good background for management of a housing project, many real estate men are deplorably lacking in understanding of social and governmental problems. Social workers, on the other hand, are likely to be deficient in business judgment.
On the basis of this statement, it would be MOST accurate to state that:

   A. Colleges and universities have failed to train qualified workers for proficiency in housing procedures
   B. Social workers are deficient in business judgment as related to the management of a housing project
   C. Real estate experience makes a person a good manager of a housing project
   D. Local housing authorities have been critical of present methods of personnel selection

KEY (CORRECT ANSWERS)

1. B
2. C
3. B
4. B
5. D

6. B
7. B
8. D
9. D
10. D

11. A
12. D
13. A
14. D
15. A

16. A
17. B
18. C
19. A
20. C

21. B
22. B
23. C
24. B
25. A

PHILOSOPHY, PRINCIPLES, PRACTICES, AND TECHNICS OF SUPERVISION, ADMINISTRATION, MANAGEMENT, AND ORGANIZATION

TABLE OF CONTENTS

	Page
MEANING OF SUPERVISION	1
THE OLD AND THE NEW SUPERVISION	1
THE EIGHT (8) BASIC PRINCIPLES OF THE NEW SUPERVISION	1
I. Principle of Responsibility	1
II. Principle of Authority	2
III. Principle of Self-Growth	2
IV. Principle of Individual Worth	2
V. Principle of Creative Leadership	2
VI. Principle of Success and Failure	2
VII. Principle of Science	3
VIII. Principle of Cooperation	3
WHAT IS ADMINISTRATION?	3
I. Practices Commonly Classed as "Supervisory"	3
II. Practices Commonly Classed as "Administrative"	3
III. Practices Commonly Classed as Both "Supervisory" and "Administrative"	4
RESPONSIBILITIES OF THE SUPERVISOR	4
COMPETENCIES OF THE SUPERVISOR	4
THE PROFESSIONAL SUPERVISOR-EMPLOYEE RELATIONSHIP	4
MINI-TEXT IN SUPERVISION, ADMINISTRATION, MANAGEMENT, AND ORGANIZATION	5
I. Brief Highlights	5
A. Levels of Management	6
B. What the Supervisor Must Learn	6
C. A Definition of Supervision	6
D. Elements of the Team Concept	6
E. Principles of Organization	6
F. The Four Important Parts of Every Job	7
G. Principles of Delegation	7
H. Principles of Effective Communications	7
I. Principles of Work Improvement	7
J. Areas of Job Improvement	7
K. Seven Key Points in Making Improvements	8

L.	Corrective Techniques for Job Improvement	8
M.	A Planning Checklist	8
N.	Five Characteristics of Good Directions	9
O.	Types of Directions	9
P.	Controls	9
Q.	Orienting the New Employee	9
R.	Checklist for Orienting New Employees	9
S.	Principles of Learning	10
T.	Causes of Poor Performance	10
U.	Four Major Steps in On-the-Job Instructions	10
V.	Employees Want Five Things	10
W.	Some Don'ts in Regard to Praise	11
X.	How to Gain Your Workers' Confidence	11
Y.	Sources of Employee Problems	11
Z.	The Supervisor's Key to Discipline	11
AA.	Five Important Processes of Management	12
BB.	When the Supervisor Fails to Plan	12
CC.	Fourteen General Principles of Management	12
DD.	Change	12

II. Brief Topical Summaries — 13

A.	Who/What is the Supervisor?	13
B.	The Sociology of Work	13
C.	Principles and Practices of Supervision	14
D.	Dynamic Leadership	14
E.	Processes for Solving Problems	15
F.	Training for Results	15
G.	Health, Safety, and Accident Prevention	16
H.	Equal Employment Opportunity	16
I.	Improving Communications	16
J.	Self-Development	17
K.	Teaching and Training	17
	1. The Teaching Process	17
	a. Preparation	17
	b. Presentation	18
	c. Summary	18
	d. Application	18
	e. Evaluation	18
	2. Teaching Methods	18
	a. Lecture	18
	b. Discussion	18
	c. Demonstration	19
	d. Performance	19
	e. Which Method to Use	19

PHILOSOPHY, PRINCIPLES, PRACTICES, AND TECHNICS
OF
SUPERVISION, ADMINISTRATION, MANAGEMENT, AND ORGANIZATION

MEANING OF SUPERVISION

The extension of the democratic philosophy has been accompanied by an extension in the scope of supervision. Modern leaders and supervisors no longer think of supervision in the narrow sense of being confined chiefly to visiting employees, supplying materials, or rating the staff. They regard supervision as being intimately related to all the concerned agencies of society, they speak of the supervisor's function in terms of "growth," rather than the "improvement" of employees.

This modern concept of supervision may be defined as follows: Supervision is leadership and the development of leadership within groups which are cooperatively engaged in inspection, research, training, guidance, and evaluation.

THE OLD AND THE NEW SUPERVISION

TRADITIONAL
1. Inspection
2. Focused on the employee
3. Visitation
4. Random and haphazard
5. Imposed and authoritarian
6. One person usually

MODERN
1. Study and analysis
2. Focused on aims, materials, methods, supervisors, employees, environment
3. Demonstrations, intervisitation, workshops, directed reading, bulletins, etc.
4. Definitely organized and planned (scientific)
5. Cooperative and democratic
6. Many persons involved (creative)

THE EIGHT (8) BASIC PRINCIPLES OF THE NEW SUPERVISION

I. Principle of Responsibility
Authority to act and responsibility for acting must be joined.
   A. If you give responsibility, give authority.
   B. Define employee duties clearly.
   C. Protect employees from criticism by others.
   D. Recognize the rights as well as obligations of employees.
   E. Achieve the aims of a democratic society insofar as it is possible within the area of your work.
   F. Establish a situation favorable to training and learning.
   G. Accept ultimate responsibility for everything done in your section, unit, office, division, department.
   H. Good administration and good supervision are inseparable.

II. Principle of Authority
The success of the supervisor is measured by the extent to which the power of authority is not used.
   A. Exercise simplicity and informality in supervision
   B. Use the simplest machinery of supervision
   C. If it is good for the organization as a whole, it is probably justified.
   D. Seldom be arbitrary or authoritative.
   E. Do not base your work on the power of position or of personality.
   F. Permit and encourage the free expression of opinions.

III. Principle of Self-Growth
The success of the supervisor is measured by the extent to which, and the speed with which, he is no longer needed.
   A. Base criticism on principles, not on specifics.
   B. Point out higher activities to employees.
   C. Train for self-thinking by employees to meet new situations.
   D. Stimulate initiative, self-reliance, and individual responsibility
   E. Concentrate on stimulating the growth of employees rather than on removing defects.

IV. Principle of Individual Worth
Respect for the individual is a paramount consideration in supervision.
   A. Be human and sympathetic in dealing with employees.
   B. Don't nag about things to be done.
   C. Recognize the individual differences among employees and seek opportunities to permit best expression of each personality.

V. Principle of Creative Leadership
The best supervision is that which is not apparent to the employee.
   A. Stimulate, don't drive employees to creative action.
   B. Emphasize doing good things.
   C. Encourage employees to do what they do best.
   D. Do not be too greatly concerned with details of subject or method.
   E. Do not be concerned exclusively with immediate problems and activities.
   F. Reveal higher activities and make them both desired and maximally possible.
   G. Determine procedures in the light of each situation but see that these are derived from a sound basic philosophy.
   H. Aid, inspire, and lead so as to liberate the creative spirit latent in all good employees.

VI. Principle of Success and Failure
There are no unsuccessful employees, only unsuccessful supervisors who have failed to give proper leadership.
   A. Adapt suggestions to the capacities, attitudes, and prejudices of employees.
   B. Be gradual, be progressive, be persistent.
   C. Help the employee find the general principle; have the employee apply his own problem to the general principle.
   D. Give adequate appreciation for good work and honest effort.
   E. Anticipate employee difficulties and help to prevent them.
   F. Encourage employees to do the desirable things they will do anyway.
   G. Judge your supervision by the results it secures.

VII. Principle of Science
Successful supervision is scientific, objective, and experimental. It is based on facts, not on prejudices.
- A. Be cumulative in results.
- B. Never divorce your suggestions from the goals of training.
- C. Don't be impatient of results.
- D. Keep all matters on a professional, not a personal, level.
- E. Do not be concerned exclusively with immediate problems and activities.
- F. Use objective means of determining achievement and rating where possible.

VIII. Principle of Cooperation
Supervision is a cooperative enterprise between supervisor and employee.
- A. Begin with conditions as they are.
- B. Ask opinions of all involved when formulating policies.
- C. Organization is as good as its weakest link.
- D. Let employees help to determine policies and department programs.
- E. Be approachable and accessible—physically and mentally.
- F. Develop pleasant social relationships.

WHAT IS ADMINISTRATION

Administration is concerned with providing the environment, the material facilities, and the operational procedures that will promote the maximum growth and development of supervisors and employees. (Organization is an aspect and a concomitant of administration.)

There is no sharp line of demarcation between supervision and administration; these functions are intimately interrelated and, often, overlapping. They are complementary activities.

I. Practices Commonly Classed as "Supervisory"
- A. Conducting employees' conferences
- B. Visiting sections, units, offices, divisions, departments
- C. Arranging for demonstrations
- D. Examining plans
- E. Suggesting professional reading
- F. Interpreting bulletins
- G. Recommending in-service training courses
- H. Encouraging experimentation
- I. Appraising employee morale
- J. Providing for intervisitation

II. Practices Commonly Classified as "Administrative"
- A. Management of the office
- B. Arrangement of schedules for extra duties
- C. Assignment of rooms or areas
- D. Distribution of supplies
- E. Keeping records and reports
- F. Care of audio-visual materials
- G. Keeping inventory records
- H. Checking record cards and books

I. Programming special activities
   J. Checking on the attendance and punctuality of employees

III. Practices Commonly Classified as Both "Supervisory" and "Administrative"
   A. Program construction
   B. Testing or evaluating outcomes
   C. Personnel accounting
   D. Ordering instructional materials

RESPONSIBILITIES OF THE SUPERVISOR

A person employed in a supervisory capacity must constantly be able to improve his own efficiency and ability. He represent the employer to the employees and only continuous self-examination can make him a capable supervisor.

Leadership and training are the supervisor's responsibility. An efficient working unit is one in which the employees work with the supervisor. It is his job to bring out the best in his employees. He must always be relaxed, courteous, and calm in his association with his employees. Their feelings are important, and a harsh attitude does not develop the most efficient employees.

COMPETENCES OF THE SUPERVISOR

   I. Complete knowledge of the duties and responsibilities of his position.
   II. To be able to organize a job, plan ahead, and carry through.
   III. To have self-confidence and initiative.
   IV. To be able to handle the unexpected situation and make quick decisions.
   V. To be able to properly train subordinates in the positions they are best suited for.
   VI. To be able to keep good human relations among his subordinates.
   VII. To be able to keep good human relations between his subordinates and himself and to earn their respect and trust.

THE PROFESSIONAL SUPERVISOR-EMPLOYEE RELATIONSHIP

There are two kinds of efficiency: one kind is only apparent and is produced in organizations through the exercise of mere discipline; this is but a simulation of the second, or true, efficiency which springs from spontaneous cooperation. If you are a manager, no matter how great or small your responsibility, it is your job, in the final analysis, to create and develop this involuntary cooperation among the people whom you supervise. For, no matter how powerful a combination of money, machines, and materials a company may have, this is a dead and sterile thing without a team of willing, thinking, and articulate people to guide it.

The following 21 points are presented as indicative of the exemplary basic relationship that should exist between supervisor and employee:

1. Each person wants to be liked and respected by his fellow employee and wants to be treated with consideration and respect by his superior.
2. The most competent employee will make an error. However, in a unit where good relations exist between the supervisor and his employees, tenseness and fear do not exist. Thus, errors are not hidden or covered up, and the efficiency of a unit is not impaired.

3. Subordinates resent rules, regulations, or orders that are unreasonable or unexplained.
4. Subordinates are quick to resent unfairness, harshness, injustices, and favoritism.
5. An employee will accept responsibility if he knows that he will be complimented for a job well done, and not too harshly chastised for failure; that his supervisor will check the cause of the failure, and, if it was the supervisor's fault, he will assume the blame therefore. If it was the employee's fault, his supervisor will explain the correct method or means of handling the responsibility.
6. An employee wants to receive credit for a suggestion he has made, that is used. If a suggestion cannot be used, the employee is entitled to an explanation. The supervisor should not say "no" and close the subject.
7. Fear and worry slow up a worker's ability. Poor working environment can impair his physical and mental health. A good supervisor avoids forceful methods, threats, and arguments to get a job done.
8. A forceful supervisor is able to train his employees individually and as a team, and is able to motivate them in the proper channels.
9. A mature supervisor is able to properly evaluate his subordinates and to keep them happy and satisfied.
10. A sensitive supervisor will never patronize his subordinates.
11. A worthy supervisor will respect his employees' confidences.
12. Definite and clear-cut responsibilities should be assigned to each executive.
13. Responsibility should always be coupled with corresponding authority.
14. No change should be made in the scope or responsibilities of a position without a definite understanding to that effect on the part of all persons concerned.
15. No executive or employee, occupying a single position in the organization, should be subject to definite orders from more than one source.
16. Orders should never be given to subordinates over the head of a responsible executive. Rather than do this, the officer in question should be supplanted.
17. Criticisms of subordinates should, whoever possible, be made privately, and in no case should a subordinate be criticized in the presence of executives or employees of equal or lower rank.
18. No dispute or difference between executives or employees as to authority or responsibilities should be considered too trivial for prompt and careful adjudication.
19. Promotions, wage changes, and disciplinary action should always be approved by the executive immediately superior to the one directly responsible.
20. No executive or employee should ever be required, or expected, to be at the same time an assistant to, and critic of, another.
21. Any executive whose work is subject to regular inspection should, wherever practicable, be given the assistance and facilities necessary to enable him to maintain an independent check of the quality of his work.

MINI-TEXT IN SUPERVISION, ADMINISTRATION, MANAGEMENT, AND ORGANIZATION

I. Brief Highlights

Listed concisely and sequentially are major headings and important data in the field for quick recall and review.

A. Levels of Management
Any organization of some size has several levels of management. In terms of a ladder, the levels are:

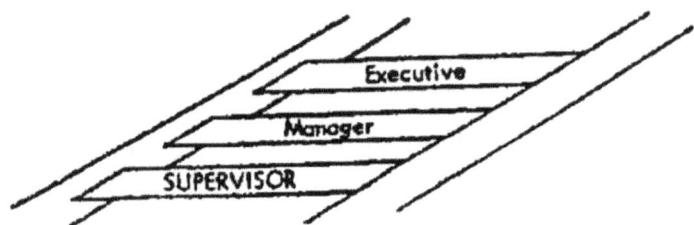

The first level is very important because it is the beginning point of management leadership.

B. What the Supervisor Must Learn
A supervisor must learn to:
1. Deal with people and their differences
2. Get the job done through people
3. Recognize the problems when they exist
4. Overcome obstacles to good performance
5. Evaluate the performance of people
6. Check his own performance in terms of accomplishment

C. A Definition of Supervisor
The term supervisor means any individual having authority, in the interests of the employer, to hire, transfer, suspend, lay-off, recall, promote, discharge, assign, reward, or discipline other employees or responsibility to direct them, or to adjust their grievances, or effectively to recommend such action, if, in connection with the foregoing, exercise of such authority is not of a merely routine or clerical nature but requires the use of independent judgment.

D. Elements of the Team Concept
What is involved in teamwork? The component parts are:
1. Members
2. A leader
3. Goals
4. Plans
5. Cooperation
6. Spirit

E. Principles of Organization
1. A team member must know what his job is.
2. Be sure that the nature and scope of a job are understood.
3. Authority and responsibility should be carefully spelled out.
4. A supervisor should be permitted to make the maximum number of decisions affecting his employees.
5. Employees should report to only one supervisor.
6. A supervisor should direct only as many employees as he can handle effectively.
7. An organization plan should be flexible.

8. Inspection and performance of work should be separate.
9. Organizational problems should receive immediate attention.
10. Assign work in line with ability and experience.

F. The Four Important Parts of Every Job
1. Inherent in every job is the *accountability* for results.
2. A second set of factors in every job is *responsibilities*.
3. Along with duties and responsibilities one must have the *authority* to act within certain limits without obtaining permission to proceed.
4. No job exists in a vacuum. The supervisor is surrounded by key *relationships*.

G. Principles of Delegation
Where work is delegated for the first time, the supervisor should think in terms of these questions:
1. Who is best qualified to do this?
2. Can an employee improve his abilities by doing this?
3. How long should an employee spend on this?
4. Are there any special problems for which he will need guidance?
5. How broad a delegation can I make?

H. Principles of Effective Communications
1. Determine the media.
2. To whom directed?
3. Identification and source authority.
4. Is communication understood?

I. Principles of Work Improvement
1. Most people usually do only the work which is assigned to them.
2. Workers are likely to fit assigned work into the time available to perform it.
3. A good workload usually stimulates output.
4. People usually do their best work when they know that results will be reviewed or inspected.
5. Employees usually feel that someone else is responsible for conditions of work, workplace layout, job methods, type of tools/equipment, and other such factors.
6. Employees are usually defensive about their job security.
7. Employees have natural resistance to change.
8. Employees can support or destroy a supervisor.
9. A supervisor usually earns the respect of his people through his personal example of diligence and efficiency.

J. Areas of Job Improvement
The areas of job improvement are quite numerous, but the most common ones which a supervisor can identify and utilize are:
1. Departmental layout
2. Flow of work
3. Workplace layout
4. Utilization of manpower
5. Work methods
6. Materials handling

7. Utilization
8. Motion economy

K. Seven Key Points in Making Improvements
   1. Select the job to be improved
   2. Study how it is being done now
   3. Question the present method
   4. Determine actions to be taken
   5. Chart proposed method
   6. Get approval and apply
   7. Solicit worker participation

l. Corrective Techniques of Job Improvement
   Specific Problems
   1. Size of workload
   2. Inability to meet schedules
   3. Strain and fatigue
   4. Improper use of men and skills
   5. Waste, poor quality, unsafe conditions
   6. Bottleneck conditions that hinder output
   7. Poor utilization of equipment and machine
   8. Efficiency and productivity of labor

   General Improvement
   1. Departmental layout
   2. Flow of work
   3. Work plan layout
   4. Utilization of manpower
   5. Work methods
   6. Materials handling
   7. Utilization of equipment
   8. Motion economy

   Corrective Techniques
   1. Study with scale model
   2. Flow chart study
   3. Motion analysis
   4. Comparison of units produced to standard allowance
   5. Methods analysis
   6. Flow chart and equipment study
   7. Down time vs. running time
   8. Motion analysis

M. A Planning Checklist
   1. Objectives
   2. Controls
   3. Delegations
   4. Communications
   5. Resources
   6. Manpower

7. Equipment
8. Supplies and materials
9. Utilization of time
10. Safety
11. Money
12. Work
13. Timing of improvements

N. Five Characteristics of Good Directions
In order to get results, directions must be:
1. Possible of accomplishment
2. Agreeable with worker interests
3. Related to mission
4. Planned and complete
5. Unmistakably clear

O. Types of Directions
1. Demands or direct orders
2. Requests
3. Suggestion or implication
4. volunteering

P. Controls
A typical listing of the overall areas in which the supervisor should establish controls might be:
1. Manpower
2. Materials
3. Quality of work
4. Quantity of work
5. Time
6. Space
7. Money
8. Methods

Q. Orienting the New Employee
1. Prepare for him
2. Welcome the new employee
3. Orientation for the job
4. Follow-up

R. Checklist for Orienting New Employees   Yes   No
1. Do you appreciate the feelings of new employees when they first report for work?   ___   ___
2. Are you aware of the fact that the new employee must make a big adjustment to his job?   ___   ___
3. Have you given him good reasons for liking the job and the organization?   ___   ___
4. Have you prepared for his first day on the job?   ___   ___
5. Did you welcome him cordially and make him feel needed?   ___   ___

		Yes	No

6. Did you establish rapport with him so that he feels free to talk and discuss matters with you? ___ ___
7. Did you explain his job to him and his relationship to you? ___ ___
8. Does he know that his work will be evaluated periodically on a basis that is fair and objective? ___ ___
9. Did you introduce him to his fellow workers in such a way that they are likely to accept him? ___ ___
10. Does he know what employee benefits he will receive? ___ ___
11. Does he understand the importance of being on the job and what to do if he must leave his duty station? ___ ___
12. Has he been impressed with the importance of accident prevention and safe practice? ___ ___
13. Does he generally know his way around the department? ___ ___
14. Is he under the guidance of a sponsor who will teach the right way of doing things? ___ ___
15. Do you plan to follow-up so that he will continue to adjust successfully to his job? ___ ___

S. Principles of Learning
1. Motivation
2. Demonstration or explanation
3. Practice

T. Causes of Poor Performance
1. Improper training for job
2. Wrong tools
3. Inadequate directions
4. Lack of supervisory follow-up
5. Poor communications
6. Lack of standards of performance
7. Wrong work habits
8. Low morale
9. Other

U. Four Major Steps in On-The-Job Instruction
1. Prepare the worker
2. Present the operation
3. Tryout performance
4. Follow-up

V. Employees Want Five Things
1. Security
2. Opportunity
3. Recognition
4. Inclusion
5. Expression

W. Some Don'ts in Regard to Praise
1. Don't praise a person for something he hasn't done.
2. Don't praise a person unless you can be sincere.
3. Don't be sparing in praise just because your superior withholds it from you.
4. Don't let too much time elapse between good performance and recognition of it

X. How to Gain Your Workers' Confidence
Methods of developing confidence include such things as:
1. Knowing the interests, habits, hobbies of employees
2. Admitting your own inadequacies
3. Sharing and telling of confidence in others
4. Supporting people when they are in trouble
5. Delegating matters that can be well handled
6. Being frank and straightforward about problems and working conditions
7. Encouraging others to bring their problems to you
8. Taking action on problems which impede worker progress

Y. Sources of Employee Problems
On-the-job causes might be such things as:
1. A feeling that favoritism is exercised in assignments
2. Assignment of overtime
3. An undue amount of supervision
4. Changing methods or systems
5. Stealing of ideas or trade secrets
6. Lack of interest in job
7. Threat of reduction in force
8. Ignorance or lack of communications
9. Poor equipment
10. Lack of knowing how supervisor feels toward employee
11. Shift assignments

Off-the-job problems might have to do with:
1. Health
2. Finances
3. Housing
4. Family

Z. The Supervisor's Key to Discipline
There are several key points about discipline which the supervisor should keep in mind:
1. Job discipline is one of the disciplines of life and is directed by the supervisor.
2. It is more important to correct an employee fault than to fix blame for it.
3. Employee performance is affected by problems both on the job and off.
4. Sudden or abrupt changes in behavior can be indications of important employee problems.
5. Problems should be dealt with as soon as possible after they are identified.
6. The attitude of the supervisor may have more to do with solving problems than the techniques of problem solving.
7. Correction of employee behavior should be resorted to only after the supervisor is sure that training or counseling will not be helpful.

8. Be sure to document your disciplinary actions.
9. Make sure that you are disciplining on the basis of facts rather than personal feelings.
10. Take each disciplinary step in order, being careful not to make snap judgments, or decisions based on impatience.

AA. Five Important Processes of Management
1. Planning
2. Organizing
3. Scheduling
4. Controlling
5. Motivating

BB. When the Supervisor Fails to Plan
1. Supervisor creates impression of not knowing his job
2. May lead to excessive overtime
3. Job runs itself—supervisor lacks control
4. Deadlines and appointments missed
5. Parts of the work go undone
6. Work interrupted by emergencies
7. Sets a bad example
8. Uneven workload creates peaks and valleys
9. Too much time on minor details at expense of more important tasks

CC. Fourteen General Principles of Management
1. Division of work
2. Authority and responsibility
3. Discipline
4. Unity of command
5. Unity of direction
6. Subordination of individual interest to general interest
7. Remuneration of personnel
8. Centralization
9. Scalar chain
10. Order
11. Equity
12. Stability of tenure of personnel
13. Initiative
14. Esprit de corps

DD. Change

Bringing about change is perhaps attempted more often, and yet less well understood, than anything else the supervisor does. How do people generally react to change? (People tend to resist change that is imposed upon them by other individuals or circumstances.

Change is characteristic of every situation. It is a part of every real endeavor where the efforts of people are concerned.

1. Why do people resist change?
   People may resist change because of:
   a. Fear of the unknown
   b. Implied criticism
   c. Unpleasant experiences in the past
   d. Fear of loss of status
   e. Threat to the ego
   f. Fear of loss of economic stability

2. How can we best overcome the resistance to change?
   In initiating change, take these steps:
   a. Get ready to sell
   b. Identify sources of help
   c. Anticipate objections
   d. Sell benefits
   e. Listen in depth
   f. Follow up

II. Brief Topical Summaries

   A. Who/What is the Supervisor?
      1. The supervisor is often called the "highest level employee and the lowest level manager."
      2. A supervisor is a member of both management and the work group. He acts as a bridge between the two.
      3. Most problems in supervision are in the area of human relations, or people problems.
      4. Employees expect: Respect, opportunity to learn and to advance, and a sense of belonging, and so forth.
      5. Supervisors are responsible for directing people and organizing work. Planning is of paramount importance.
      6. A position description is a set of duties and responsibilities inherent to a given position.
      7. It is important to keep the position description up-to-date and to provide each employee with his own copy.

   B. The Sociology of Work
      1. People are alike in many ways; however, each individual is unique.
      2. The supervisor is challenged in getting to know employee differences. Acquiring skills in evaluating individuals is an asset.
      3. Maintaining meaningful working relationships in the organization is of great importance.
      4. The supervisor has an obligation to help individuals to develop to their fullest potential.
      5. Job rotation on a planned basis helps to build versatility and to maintain interest and enthusiasm in work groups.
      6. Cross training (job rotation) provides backup skills.

7. The supervisor can help reduce tension by maintaining a sense of humor, providing guidance to employees, and by making reasonable and timely decisions. Employees respond favorably to working under reasonably predictable circumstances.
8. Change is characteristic of all managerial behavior. The supervisor must adjust to changes in procedures, new methods, technological changes, and to a number of new and sometimes challenging situations.
9. To overcome the natural tendency for people to resist change, the supervisor should become more skillful in initiating change.

C. Principles and Practices of Supervision
1. Employees should be required to answer to only one superior.
2. A supervisor can effectively direct only a limited number of employees, depending upon the complexity, variety, and proximity of the jobs involved.
3. The organizational chart presents the organization in graphic form. It reflects lines of authority and responsibility as well as interrelationships of units within the organization.
4. Distribution of work can be improved through an analysis using the "Work Distribution Chart."
5. The "Work Distribution Chart" reflects the division of work within a unit in understandable form.
6. When related tasks are given to an employee, he has a better chance of increasing his skills through training.
7. The individual who is given the responsibility for tasks must also be given the appropriate authority to insure adequate results.
8. The supervisor should delegate repetitive, routine work. Preparation of recurring reports, maintaining leave and attendance records are some examples.
9. Good discipline is essential to good task performance. Discipline is reflected in the actions of employees on the job in the absence of supervision.
10. Disciplinary action may have to be taken when the positive aspects of discipline have failed. Reprimand, warning, and suspension are examples of disciplinary action.
11. If a situation calls for a reprimand, be sure it is deserved and remember it is to be done in private.

D. Dynamic Leadership
1. A style is a personal method or manner of exerting influence.
2. Authoritarian leaders often see themselves as the source of power and authority.
3. The democratic leader often perceives the group as the source of authority and power.
4. Supervisors tend to do better when using the pattern of leadership that is most natural for them.
5. Social scientists suggest that the effective supervisor use the leadership style that best fits the problem or circumstances involved.
6. All four styles—telling, selling, consulting, joining—have their place. Using one does not preclude using the other at another time.

7. The theory X point of view assumes that the average person dislikes work, will avoid it whenever possible, and must be coerced to achieve organizational objectives.
8. The theory Y point of view assumes that the average person considers work to be a natural as play, and, when the individual is committed, he requires little supervision or direction to accomplish desired objectives.
9. The leader's basic assumptions concerning human behavior and human nature affect his actions, decisions, and other managerial practices.
10. Dissatisfaction among employees is often present, but difficult to isolate. The supervisor should seek to weaken dissatisfaction by keeping promises, being sincere and considerate, keeping employees informed, and so forth.
11. Constructive suggestions should be encouraged during the natural progress of the work.

E. Processes for Solving Problems
1. People find their daily tasks more meaningful and satisfying when they can improve them.
2. The causes of problems, or the key factors, are often hidden in the background. Ability to solve problems often involves the ability to isolate them from their backgrounds. There is some substance to the cliché that some persons "can't see the forest for the trees."
3. New procedures are often developed from old ones. Problems should be broken down into manageable parts. New ideas can be adapted from old one.
4. People think differently in problem-solving situations. Using a logical, patterned approach is often useful. One approach found to be useful includes these steps:
   a. Define the problem
   b. Establish objectives
   c. Get the facts
   d. Weigh and decide
   e. Take action
   f. Evaluate action

F. Training for Results
1. Participants respond best when they feel training is important to them.
2. The supervisor has responsibility for the training and development of those who report to him.
3. When training is delegated to others, great care must be exercised to insure the trainer has knowledge, aptitude, and interest for his work as a trainer.
4. Training (learning) of some type goes on continually. The most successful supervisor makes certain the learning contributes in a productive manner to operational goals.
5. New employees are particularly susceptible to training. Older employees facing new job situations require specific training, as well as having need for development and growth opportunities.
6. Training needs require continuous monitoring.
7. The training officer of an agency is a professional with a responsibility to assist supervisors in solving training problems.

8. Many of the self-development steps important to the supervisor's own growth are equally important to the development of peers and subordinates. Knowledge of these is important when the supervisor consults with others on development and growth opportunities.

G. Health, Safety, and Accident Prevention
1. Management-minded supervisors take appropriate measures to assist employees in maintaining health and in assuring safe practices in the work environment.
2. Effective safety training and practices help to avoid injury and accidents.
3. Safety should be a management goal. All infractions of safety which are observed should be corrected without exception.
4. Employees' safety attitude, training and instruction, provision of safe tools and equipment, supervision, and leadership are considered highly important factors which contribute to safety and which can be influenced directly by supervisors.
5. When accidents do occur, they should be investigated promptly for very important reasons, including the fact that information which is gained can be used to prevent accidents in the future.

H. Equal Employment Opportunity
1. The supervisor should endeavor to treat all employees fairly, without regard to religion, race, sex, or national origin.
2. Groups tend to reflect the attitude of the leader. Prejudice can be detected even in very subtle form. Supervisors must strive to create a feeling of mutual respect and confidence in every employee.
3. Complete utilization of all human resources is a national goal. Equitable consideration should be accorded women in the work force, minority-group members, the physically and mentally handicapped, and the older employee. The important question is: "Who can do the job?"
4. Training opportunities, recognition for performance, overtime assignments, promotional opportunities, and all other personnel actions are to be handled on an equitable basis.

I. Improving Communications
1. Communications is achieving understanding between the sender and the receiver of a message. It also means sharing information—the creation of understanding.
2. Communication is basic to all human activity. Words are means of conveying meanings; however, real meanings are in people.
3. There are very practical differences in the effectiveness of one-way, impersonal, and two-way communications. Words spoken face-to-face are better understood. Telephone conversations are effective, but lack the rapport of person-to-person exchanges. The whole person communicates.
4. Cooperation and communication in an organization go hand in hand. When there is a mutual respect between people, spelling out rules and procedures for communicating is unnecessary.
5. There are several barriers to effective communications. These include failure to listen with respect and understanding, lack of skill in feedback, and misinterpreting the meanings of words used by the speaker. It is also common

practice to listen to what we want to hear, and tune out things we do not want to hear.
6. Communication is management's chief problem. The supervisor should accept the challenge to communicate more effectively and to improve interagency and intra-agency communications.
7. The supervisor may often plan for and conduct meetings. The planning phase is critical and may determine the success or the failure of a meeting.
8. Speaking before groups usually requires extra effort. Stage fright may never disappear completely, but it can be controlled.

J. Self-Development
1. Every employee is responsible for his own self-development.
2. Toastmaster and toastmistress clubs offer opportunities to improve skills in oral communications.
3. Planning for one's own self-development is of vital importance. Supervisors know their own strengths and limitations better than anyone else.
4. Many opportunities are open to aid the supervisor in his developmental efforts, including job assignments; training opportunities, both governmental and non-governmental—to include universities and professional conferences and seminars.
5. Programmed instruction offers a means of studying at one's own rate.
6. Where difficulties may arise from a supervisor's being away from his work for training, he may participate in televised home study or correspondence courses to meet his self-development needs.

K. Teaching and Training
1. The Teaching Process
Teaching is encouraging and guiding the learning activities of students toward established goals. In most cases this process consists of five steps: preparation, presentation, summarization, evaluation, and application.

   a. Preparation
   Preparation is two-fold in nature; that of the supervisor and the employee. Preparation by the supervisor is absolutely essential to success. He must know what, when, where, how, and whom he will teach. Some of the factors that should be considered are:
   1) The objectives
   2) The materials needed
   3) The methods to be used
   4) Employee participation
   5) Employee interest
   6) Training aids
   7) Evaluation
   8) Summarization

   Employee preparation consists in preparing the employee to receive the material. Probably the most important single factor in the preparation of the employee is arousing and maintaining his interest. He must know the objectives of the training, why he is there, how the material can be used, and its importance to him.

b. Presentation
   In presentation, have a carefully designed plan and follow it. The plan should be accurate and complete, yet flexible enough to meet situations as they arise. The method of presentation will be determined by the particular situation and objectives.

c. Summary
   A summary should be made at the end of every training unit and program. In addition, there may be internal summaries depending on the nature of the material being taught. The important thing is that the trainee must always be able to understand how each part of the new material relates to the whole.

d. Application
   The supervisor must arrange work so the employee will be given a chance to apply new knowledge or skills while the material is still clear in his mind and interest is high. The trainee does not really know whether he has learned the material until he has been given a chance to apply it. If the material is not applied, it loses most of its value.

e. Evaluation
   The purpose of all training is to promote learning. To determine whether the training has been a success or failure, the supervisor must evaluate this learning.
   In the broadest sense, evaluation includes all the devices, methods, skills, and techniques used by the supervisor to keep himself and the employees informed as to their progress toward the objectives they are pursuing. The extent to which the employee has mastered the knowledge, skills, and abilities, or changed his attitudes, as determined by the program objectives, is the extent to which instruction has succeeded or failed.
   Evaluation should not be confined to the end of the lesson, day, or program but should be used continuously. We shall note later the way this relates to the rest of the teaching process.

2. Teaching Methods
   A teaching method is a pattern of identifiable student and instructor activity used in presenting training material.
   All supervisors are faced with the problem of deciding which method should be used at a given time.

   a. Lecture
      The lecture is direct oral presentation of material by the supervisor. The present trend is to place less emphasis on the trainer's activity and more on that of the trainee.

   b. Discussion
      Teaching by discussion or conference involves using questions and other techniques to arouse interest and focus attention upon certain areas, and by doing so creating a learning situation. This can be one of the most

valuable methods because it gives the employees an opportunity to express their ideas and pool their knowledge.

c. Demonstration
The demonstration is used to teach how something works or how to do something. It can be used to show a principle or what the results of a series of actions will be. A well-staged demonstration is particularly effective because it shows proper methods of performance in a realistic manner.

d. Performance
Performance is one of the most fundamental of all learning techniques or teaching methods. The trainee may be able to tell how a specific operation should be performed but he cannot be sure he knows how to perform the operation until he has done so.
As with all methods, there are certain advantages and disadvantages to each method.

e. Which Method to Use
Moreover, there are other methods and techniques of teaching. It is difficult to use any method without other methods entering into it. In any learning situation, a combination of methods is usually more effective than any one method alone.

Finally, evaluation must be integrated into the other aspects of the teaching-learning process.

It must be used in the motivation of the trainees; it must be used to assist in developing understanding during the training; and it must be related to employee application of the results of training.

This is distinctly the role of the supervisor.

TRENDS IN HOUSING

CONTENTS

		Page
I.	The History of Housing	1
II.	Trends in Housing Inspection	4
III.	Role of Health Agencies in Housing	6
IV.	Summary	6

TRENDS IN HOUSING

Members of countless communities throughout America are raising critical questions about the adequacy and effectiveness of local housing code enforcement programs. These critics feel deep concern over the fact that 1966 found "some four million urban families living in homes of such disrepair as to violate decent housing standards." For this reason, they insist everything possible be done to guarantee that present and future inspection efforts lead to rapid and adequate upgrading of the substandard but salvageable housing in each community and that the neighborhoods be made more desirable places in which to live.

In order to meet these demands effectively, inspectors of housing and their supervisors should first acquaint themselves with the origin of public concern about housing problems; the past, present, and new approaches to housing code administration; the expanded role of the inspection function in the neighborhood improvement effort; and the general nature of their role and responsibilities

I. The History of Housing

The first public policies on housing in this country were established during the Colonial period. Many of the early settlers built houses with wooden chimneys and thatched roofs which were the causes of frequent fires. Consequently, several of the colonies passed regulations prohibiting these. One of the first was the Plymouth Colony, which in 1626 passed a law stipulating that new houses should not be thatched but roofed with either board or pale and the like. In 1648 wooden or plastered chimneys were prohibited on new houses in New Amsterdam, and chimneys on existing houses were decreed to be inspected regularly. In Charlestown in 1740, following a disastrous fire, the general assembly passed an act that declared that all buildings should be of brick or stone, that all "tall" wooded houses must be pulled down by 1745, and that the use of wood was to be confined to window frames, shutters, and to exterior work. This law was obviously unenforceable because, as we learn from other publications during that period, more Charlestown houses were made of timber than of brick.

Social control over housing was exerted in other ways. Early settlers in Pennsylvania frequently dug caves out of the banks of the Delaware River and used these as primitive-type dwellings. Some of these shelters were still in use as late as 1687 when the Provincial Council ordered inhabitants to provide for themselves other habitations, in order to have the said caves or houses destroyed. In some New England communities, around the turn of the 18th century, standards were raised considerably higher by local ordinances. In East Greenwich, it had been the custom to build houses 14 feet square with posts 9 feet high; in 1727 the town voted that houses shall be built 18 feet square with-posts 15 feet high with chimneys of stone or brick as before.

During the early days of this country, basic sanitation was very poor, primarily because outdoor privies served as the general means of sewage disposal. The principal problems created by the use of these privies involved their nearness to the streets and their easy accessibility to hogs and goats. In 1652, Boston prohibited the building of privies within 12 feet of the street. The Dutch of New Amsterdam in 1657 prohibited the throwing of rubbish and filth into the streets or canal and required the householders to keep the streets clean and orderly.

After the early Colonial period we pass into an era of very rapid metropolitan growth along the eastern seashore. This growth was due largely to the immigration of people from Europe. Frequently these immigrants arrived without money or jobs and were forced to move in with friends or relatives. This led to severe overcrowding. Most of the information available pertains to New York City, because the situation there was worse than that in any other city in the country. It received the majority of the immigrants, many of whom were unable to move beyond the city. The most serious housing problems began in New York about 1840 when the first tenements were built. These provided such substandard housing and such unhealthy, crowded living conditions that a social reform movement was imminent in New York.

During the early part of the 19th century, the only housing control authority was that vested in the fire wardens, whose objective was to prevent fires, and the health wardens, who were charged with the enforcement of general sanitation. In 1867, with the passing of the Tenement Housing Act, New York City began to face the problem of substandard housing. This law represented the first comprehensive legislation of its kind in this country. The principal features of the act are summarized as follows: for every room occupied for sleeping in a tenement or lodging house, if it does not communicate directly with the external air, a ventilating or transom window to the neighboring room or hall; a proper fire escape on every tenement or lodging house; the roof to be kept in repair and the stairs to have bannisters; water closets or privies – at least one to every twenty occupants for all such houses; after July 1, 1867, permits for occupancy of every cellar not previously occupied as a dwelling; cleansing of every lodging house to the satisfaction of the Board of Health, which is to have access at any time; reporting of all cases of infectious disease to the Board by the owner or his agent; inspection and, if necessary, disinfection of such houses; and vacation of buildings found to be out of repair. There were also regulations governing distances between buildings, heights of rooms, and dimensions of windows. The terms "tenement house," "lodging house," and "cellar" were defined.

Although this act had some beneficial influences on overcrowding, sewage disposal, lighting, and ventilation, it did not correct the evils of crowding on lots and did not provide for adequate ventilation for inner rooms. In 1879, a second tenement act, amending the first, was passed adding restrictions on the amount of lot coverage and providing for a window opening of at least 12 square feet in every room. Several attempts in 1882, 1884, and 1895 were made to amend this original act and provide for occupancy standards, but they were relatively unenforceable. While these numerous acts remedied only slightly the serious problems of the tenements, they did show the city's acknowledgment of the problems. This public acknowledgment, however, was seldom shared by the owners of the tenements, or, in some cases, by the courts. The most famous case, in 1892, involved Trinity Church, at that time one of the largest owners of tenements in New York City. In the case, the City of New York accused Trinity Church of violating provisions of the Act of 1882 by failing to provide running water on every floor of its buildings. A district court levied a fine of $200 against the Church, which in turn appealed to the Court of Common Pleas to have the law set aside as unconstitutional. Incredibly, the court agreed unanimously to uphold the landlord's position, stating there is no evidence nor can the court judicially know that the presence and distribution of water on the several floors will conduce to the health of the occupants ... there is no necessity for legislative compulsion on a landlord to distribute water through the stories of his building; since if tenants require it, self-interest and the rivalry of competition are sufficient to secure it ... now, if it be competent for the legislature to impose an expense upon a landlord in order that tenants be furnished with water in their rooms instead of in the yard or basement, at what point must this police power pause? ... a conclusion contrary to the present decision would involve the essential principle of that species of socialism under the regime of which the individual disappears and is absorbed by a collective being called the 'state', a principle utterly repugnant to the spirit of our political system and necessarily fatal to our form of liberty. Fortunately, 3 years later, the city health department was granted an appeal from the court order, and eventually the constitutionality of the law was upheld.

Jacob A. Riis, Lawrence Veiller, and others did much during this period to champion the cause of better living conditions. Their efforts resulted in the Tenement House Act of 1901, a milestone in housing and an extremely comprehensive document for its time. It began with concise definitions of certain terms that were to become important in court actions. It contained provisions for protection from fire, requiring that every tenement erected thereafter, and exceeding 60 feet in height, should be fireproof. In addition, there were specific provisions regarding fire escapes on both new and existing houses. More light and ventilation were required; coverage was restricted to not more than 70 percent on interior lots and 90 percent on corner lots. There were special provisions governing rear yards, inner courts, and buildings on the same lot with the tenement house. At least one window of specified dimensions was required for every room, including the bathroom. Minimum size of rooms was specified as were certain characteristics for public halls. Significantly included were provisions concerning planning for the individual apartments in order to assure privacy. One of the most important provisions of the Tenement Act was the requirement for running water and water closets in each apartment in new tenement houses. Special attention was given to basements and cellars, the law requiring not only that they be damp-proof but also that permits be obtained before they were occupied. One novel section of this act prohibited the use of any part of the building as a house of prostitution.

The basic principles and methodology established in the Tenement Act of 1901 still underlie much of the housing efforts in New York City today. Philadelphia, a city that can be compared with New York from the standpoint of age, was fortunate to have farsighted leaders in its early stage of development. Since 1909, with the establishment of the Philadelphia Housing Association, the city has had almost continual inspection and improvement.

Although Chicago is approximately two centuries younger than New York, it enacted housing legislation as early as 1889 and health legislation as early as 1881. Regulations on ventilation, light, drainage, and plumbing of dwellings were put into effect in 1896. Many of the structures, however, were built of wood, were dilapidated, and constituted serious fire hazards.

Before 1892, all government involvement in housing was at a local level. In 1892, however, the Federal Government passed a resolution authorizing investigation of slum conditions in cities containing 200,000 or more inhabitants. At that time these included the cities of Baltimore, Boston, Brooklyn, Buffalo, Chicago, Cincinnati, Cleveland, Detroit, Milwaukee, New Orleans, New York, Philadelphia, Pittsburgh, St. Louis, San Francisco, and Washington. Much controversy surrounded the involvement of the Federal Government in housing. The Commissioner of Labor was forced to write an extensive legal opinion concerning the constitutionality of expenditures by the Federal Government in this area. The result was that Congress appropriated only $20,000 to cover the expenses of this project. The lack of funds limited actual investigations to Baltimore, Chicago, New York, and Philadelphia and did not cover housing conditions in toto within these cities. Facts obtained from the investigation were very broad, covering items such as the number of saloons per number of inhabitants, number of arrests, distribution of males and females, proportion of foreign-born inhabitants, degree of illiteracy, kinds of occupations of the residents, conditions of their health, their earnings, and the number of voters.

The 20th century started off rather poorly in the area of housing. No significant housing legislation was passed until 1929 when the New York State legislature passed its Multiple Dwelling Law. This law continued the Tenement Act of New York City but replaced many provisions of the 1901 law with less strict requirements. Other cities and states followed New York State's example and permitted less strict requirements in their codes. This decreased what little emphasis there was in enforcement of building laws so that during the 1920's the cities had worked themselves into a very poor state of housing. Conditions in America declined to such a state by the 30's that President Franklin D. Roosevelt's shocking report to the people was "that one-third of the nation is ill-fed, ill-housed, and ill-clothed." With this the Federal Government launched itself extensively into the field of housing. The first Federal housing law was passed in

1934. One of the purposes of this act was to create a sounder mortgage system through the provision of a permanent system of government insurance for residential mortgages. The Federal Housing Administration was created to carry out the objectives of this act. Many other Federal laws followed: the Veterans Administration becoming involved in guaranteeing of loans, the Home Loan Bank Board, Federal National Mortgage Association, Communities Facilities Administration, Public Housing Administration, and the Public Works Administration. With the U.S. Housing Act of 1937, the Federal Government entered the area of slum clearance and urban renewal, requiring one slum dwelling to be eliminated for every new unit built under the Housing Administration program. It was not until the passage of the Housing Act of 1949 that the Federal Government entered into slum clearance on a comprehensive basis.

The many responsibilities in housing administered by various agencies within the Federal Government proved to be unwieldy. Hence, in 1966 the Department of Housing and Urban Development was created to have prime responsibilities for the Federal Government's involvement in the field of housing.

II. Trends in Housing Inspection

Historically, local provisions for the inspection of housing have been completely inadequate. Usually the function has been split among two or more agencies, and the pertinent code sections have been spread among several local ordinances.

Following the work of C.E.A. Winslow, minimum code standards were made available and resulted in the passing of housing codes. This consolidation of housing requirements resulted in the field of housing inspection. Originally much of the work was devoted to complaint and referral inspections

A Complaint and Referral Inspections

In most communities the housing inspectors are expected to center their efforts primarily on complaint and referral inspections. This approach satisfies the persons making the complaints and referrals and helps improve some of the municipality's substandard housing. However, it does little to bring about general improvements in any section of the community and actually constitutes an inefficient way of using the available inspection manpower because the men have to spend so much time traveling from one area to another. Many supervisors and inspectors realize this unsystematic method not only wastes time but also is an ineffective way of upgrading housing and curbing blight. First, on complaint inspections the inspectors are usually instructed to confine their investigations to the dwelling unit specifically involved unless the general conditions are so bad that an inspection of the entire building is deemed necessary. This means most complaint inspections are piecemeal and do not ordinarily bring entire dwellings up to code standards. Second, even though numerous complaints are unwarranted, inspectors are often given so many to check each day that they do not have time to inspect other obviously substandard houses in the vicinity of those complained about. Consequently, these "rotten apples" are left to spoil the block, while the house that has been improved stands alone.

Too often inspection agencies have found they did not have enough facts on hand about the extent and distribution of the substandard housing in their communities. Thus, they were unable to convince their superiors and the public about the inadequacy of complaint inspections as the major method of uncovering violations and checking residential blight in neighborhoods. It is the consensus of housing officials that area inspections are the most effective way of doing both. Fortunately, in the 1960's, as one city after another began developing the comprehensive community renewal plans provided for in the Housing Act of 1959, this information finally started to become available. It verified the need for systematic inspections on a neighborhood basis. Congress further emphasized the importance of this new approach by including Section 301 in the Housing Act of 1964. This required all cities engaged in urban renewal to have comprehensive area inspection programs in operation by March 1967, and thereafter, in order to remain eligible for national renewal funds.

B Neighborhood Inspection Technique

The area or neighborhood inspection technique is a more recent type of inspection and one which begins to face up to the problems of saving neighborhoods from urban blight. While this is a step forward, it is merely one of several steps required if urban blight and its associated human suffering are to be minimized or controlled.

Throughout this manual the terms "area" or "neighborhood" are used interchangeably and refer to a readily identifiable portion of a community.

Whether this consists of so many blocks, an entire neighborhood, or a section thereof, it should be of such size as to permit the local code enforcement team to inspect and systematically effect minimum housing standards within a manageable time.

This means that area inspection programs involve systematic cellar-to-roof, house-to-house, block-to-block inspections of all properties within the specific area and include all the follow-up work required to bring the substandard housing up to code standards within a reasonable period. By putting major emphasis on this type of effort instead of on the complaint-oriented approach, blight is checked and an overall upgrading of residential sections is achieved in one portion of a community after another. Thus, systematic area inspection is both a longer lasting and a much more effective method of improving housing and stabilizing property values than the traditional complaint method.

Usually a municipality combines its area work with some complaint and referral inspections. This is not objectionable so long as major emphasis is given to the area programs, and the inspectors move through the various sections of town systematically. Only in this way can a community's housing inspection program contribute adequately to the municipal efforts to upgrade all substandard housing and stem the deterioration of individual homes and neighborhoods. A percentage of the inspection force should, however, be primarily assigned to complaint and referral work so that prompt action can be taken on all cases in which the problems are too severe to await action in connection with the area inspections.

While the area-wide or neighborhood inspections will correct violations of the housing code, this is all they will accomplish. Once these neighborhoods are brought up to standard, inspectors will move on to other neighborhoods but be forced to return at a later time and repeat the process.

If a neighborhood has declined to the extent that there is a large number of housing violations, then it is obvious that something or someone or both have caused the neighborhood to deteriorate. Any effort that does not also eliminate the cause for deterioration can only be a token effort and frequently a *wasted effort*. Unless a housing program evaluates the total neighborhood for both housing violations and for environmental stresses within the neighborhood that may have caused the deterioration of housing, then the inspectional effort has not been complete.

What then are these "environmental stresses"? Environmental stresses are the elements within a neighborhood that influence the physical, mental, and emotional well-being of the occupants. They include items such as noise, glare, excessive land covering, nonresidential land uses, and extensive traffic problems. If a housing program is to be complete, these stresses must be identified and assessed. Then efforts must be made in conjunction with other departments within the city to program capital improvement budgets to alleviate or minimize these stresses.

These two types of inspection are the field involvement of the housing inspector. He must inspect not only the houses for violations but also the neighborhoods for environmental stresses. This will provide him with knowledge of physical conditions within the neighborhood. As mentioned previously, however, this is not the whole problem in most neighborhoods. Generally, the very difficult problem of the human element is involved. Many buildings and neighborhoods deteriorate because of apathy on the part of the neighborhood inhabitants. Efforts must be made to motivate the slum dweller to work towards a better living environment. Experience by the Public Health Service (PHS) in motivational training has shown it to be very effective in raising the living standards of neighborhood populations.

In summary then, a housing inspection effort should be made up of three parts: First, a neighborhood or area-wide housing inspection procedure; second, a neighborhood analysis procedure to identify, assess, and eventually control environmental stresses; and third, a program of motivational training for slum dwellers to raise the living standards of the neighborhood.

III. Role of Health Agencies in Housing

Up until the end of World War II, most local housing hygiene programs were carried on by the health departments. After World War II, health agencies began to drift away from the field of housing hygiene. This gap was filled by a variety of other city agencies including building departments, police departments, fire departments, and more recently created departments of licenses and inspections. Regardless which department administers the housing code, the health department, if it is to live up to its responsibilities of protecting the public health, must have an involvement in housing. A general statement of PHS policy is that the basic responsibility of health agencies with regard to housing is to see to it that local and state governments take action to ensure that all occupied housing meets minimum public health standards. This basic responsibility falls upon federal, state, and local health agencies alike.

Several kinds of governmental action are required. These include: (1) adoption of minimum health standards in housing, (2) conduct of a program to achieve and maintain these standards, (3) periodic evaluation of the standards to ensure their current adequacy, and (4) monitoring of the standards enforcement effort to guarantee that public health values are provided. Health agencies, in order to meet their responsibilities, must accept the role of either stimulating or carrying out these four required kinds of governmental action.

In communities that have neither standards nor program, the health agency has the responsibility of initiating both by stimulating the required governmental action. Stimulation may be direct, through elected or appointed officials, or indirect, by generating public support that will trigger official action.

IV. Summary

Several basic thoughts are contained in this chapter.

1. Housing is an old, well-established but often overlooked topic within this country. Indications are, however, that the broad field of housing will receive much more attention from the policymakers throughout the country within the coming years.

2. No single agency can eliminate urban blight. A concentrated effort of all city departments, private concerns, and political bodies must be focused on small sections (neighborhoods) to minimize or control urban blight and its associated human sufferings.

3. A housing effort cannot be successful if it is merely an inspection of houses for code compliance. There must also be a united effort to eliminate environmental stresses within the neighborhood and instill motivation in slum dwellers to desire and work towards improving their environment.